A Personal Message From God

'A True Story'
By
Jayne Schriver

All rights reserved, including the right to reproduce this book or portions thereof in any form whatsoever.

For any information;
RJS Publishing
1450 W Grand Parkway S
Suite G-259
Katy, TX 77494
www.rjspublishing.com

RJS can arrange the author for live events.

ISBN978-0615748689 (RJS)

Unless otherwise stated, scripture quotes from the New International Version Bible.

"Though your sins are like scarlet, they shall be as white as snow; though they are red as crimson, they shall be like wool. (Isaiah 1:18)

Table of Contents

Dedication	6
Introduction	7
1 3:00 A.M. Phone Call	11
2 That Little Voice Inside	19
3 In The Blink of an Eye	31
4 Shattered Hearts	41
5 The 'Visit'	57
6 Celebrate Life	69
7 Grief and Memories	81
8 Financial Tragedy	87
9 Family Tragedy	95
10 Past Demons Revealed	101
11 God's Mercy	125
12 Big Brother Knows Best	135
13 Lean on Me	149
14 Hind Sight is 20/20	159
15 First Anniversary of his Death	169
16 Wolves Howling at the Door	177
17 God's Purpose Fulfilled	185
18 My Mother's Bible	195
19 My Search for Answers	205
20 My Journey Back to God	217
21 Lessons Learned	233
About the Authors	239

Dedication

First and foremost, I would like to thank God, my Heavenly Father, for not giving up on me and for this wonderful miracle He gave me to share with others.

This book would never have made it without the help of my husband and best friend, Mike. Thank you for always being there for me and giving me the courage to tell this story.

Last, but not least, I would like to thank my 'big brother' for bringing me this personal message from God that has changed my life. He was my brother, my friend, my protector, and my hero. I pray that he will be waiting at heaven's gate for me when my work here on earth is done.

James Walker Durham

Feb. 27, 1936 – Nov. 8, 2008

Introduction

The common thread that binds us together as human beings regardless of ethnicity, religion, or geographical location is the mere knowledge that we are mortal. As far as we know, humans are the only species on earth that can actually contemplate their eventual end. Most of us have wondered what happens to us when we take that last breath of life. Therefore, that question has caused many books to be written about near death experiences, but they have all been merely 'near death' experiences. These reports have given us glimpses to the other side of the veil, but never in modern times in our western culture, to the best of my knowledge, has someone returned to give us a personal message from God Himself...*until now*.

This story is a first-hand report of a message that was delivered by someone that had completely transcended his earthly body never to return to it.

There are those that will immediately grasp the magnitude and meaning of this experience and then there will be the doubters who could never fathom such a thing happening to them or anyone they know. Messages from God and dreams of Jesus are more common place in eastern cultures where they are not so influenced by our western bias towards logic. Some theologians suspect that only those far removed from God ever have such experiences. I guess I certainly qualified for that category. I wasn't committing crimes, or abusing my children, or committing adultery, or any number of things that would qualify as sins, but I was in total denial of God's existence at this time in my life which is perhaps the greatest sin of all.

Regardless, I encourage the reader to approach this with an open heart and mind. I, too, would have considered this reported experience somewhat absurd prior to it happening to me. As a matter of fact, I would have considered myself the last person in the world to ever experience something like this. I have no logical explanation for why or how it happened. I only know that God gave me a miracle that has forever changed how I look at life and death, and it has dramatically altered the course my life has taken.

Chapter 1

October 2008

3:00 A.M. Phone Call

A phone ringing at 3:00 a.m. is never good news. That certainly was the case when my husband and I were awakened from a deep and comfortable sleep snuggled in the bedroom of our forty-four foot motorhome. My husband, half asleep, stumbled to the kitchen table to answer the cell phone that was charging there.

"Hello," I heard him say in his gruff, sleepy voice. "Hold on for a second, I'll get the phone to her." He turned on the kitchen light and came back toward the rear of the RV where I was trying to wake myself up enough to comprehend what was going on. He handed me the phone and said, "It's Jib."

With a lot of anxiety in my voice, I managed to say, "Hello."

"Jayne, I'm sorry to wake you guys up so early, but I thought you should know that Jimmy was taken to the hospital in an ambulance a few minutes ago."

"Oh No!" was all I could manage to say. "What happened?"

"He woke me up about 3:00 a.m. our time and told me he was throwing up blood," she said. I followed him into his bathroom and saw a trail of blood from his bed to the toilet which was filled with blood."

"Good grief, Jib! Was he walking and functioning ok?" I asked in a totally confused state. Jib, who was a lifelong friend of my oldest brother, had been spending almost every winter with him at his home in Florida since his divorce several years ago. She had arrived early this year because I had called her about concerns I had with Jimmy's health lately.

"Yes, he seemed all right except for the blood everywhere," she answered. "Where are you and Mike now?" she asked.

"We are in Houston…Texas," I answered. "I just talked to him yesterday and told him we would be arriving in a few days. We were going to stop by and visit my aunt and uncle on our way home, but I guess we won't do that now. We are about fifteen hours away from you if we drive straight through."

"I'm leaving right now headed to Regional Hospital where they took him, and I will call you as soon as I know something, ok?" she said.

"Please do that, Jib. Mike and I will get ourselves together, and we will be on the road headed your way. Just call me when you know something…" choking back tears, I said, "Tell him I love him, and we will be there as fast as we can."

Mike held me while I cried trying to make sense of this. I just kept thinking that I was going to wake up and find that this was just a silly dream and everything would be back to normal.

For the last few years, Mike and I had been on the road in our motorhome. We were empty-nesters, who had down-sized to a condo on the water, so it was convenient and logical that I travel with him as much as possible as he did his job. He had a great job working for an equipment company based in Houston, TX. Most people had to retire before they could hit the road in their motorhome, but we got to do it while the Company paid all the expenses.

We always planned Mike's work schedule so that we would be back in Florida, which was home for us, between Thanksgiving and New Year's. That way, we always spent the holidays with family. This year we had decided to head back to Florida the end of October because Jimmy, my oldest brother, was having some ongoing health problems that had actually started right around his birthday in 2007.

It was at that time that he was diagnosed with bladder cancer. This came as a shock to all of us. Jimmy had gone to his urologist, who was a family friend, thinking that he had a swollen prostate which is common for men his age. This particular urologist used a laser technique that he invented to take care of that problem with almost no side effects at all. After a thorough physical exam and running some test, Dr. Andrews told him that he was going to have to perform surgery because it was not what was expected at all, but bladder cancer instead.

Both the doctor and Jimmy had convinced me that it was not necessary for me to be there for that surgery, and especially because our brother John had agreed to come and stay with him during and after the surgery. My brother Lee was close by, and my son, who was a pre-med student, was just a few blocks away from the hospital where the surgery was to be performed. I felt that he could not be in better hands, and I was just a phone call away throughout the whole process. Boy was I wrong.

John arrived a few days early to be there with him as he went through all of the pre-op testing and just to keep him company in general. They had a great time doing what two aging brothers will do to keep themselves occupied. I'm sure that John was there not just out of love for his brother, but out of a sense of gratitude as well. It had been less than a year ago that Jimmy had stood watch over John's hospital bed night and day expecting him to die at any moment. John had become infected with a strain of staph infection that had spread throughout his entire body, and to make matters worse, he was allergic to the antibiotic that had been the most successful for treating it. Many of John's church family stood watch with Jimmy during this difficult time, and somehow John pulled through it and has no permanent side effects from it. His pastor explained it like this; "Guess God just didn't need a Scout Master right now." John has been a Boy Scout Master for the last thirty years and was responsible for helping dozens of boys, including his own son, achieve the rank of Eagle Scout.

    John and Jimmy arrived at the hospital admittance early that Monday morning for the scheduled surgery. My son, Michael, met them there as well. Everything seemed to be going smoothly. They finally gave the pre-anesthesia to Jimmy in his IV and wheeled him into the operating room. Several hours later, John and Michael were pacing the floor wondering what could possibly be taking so long. This was supposed to be relatively quick. Dr. Andrews was going to come out and explain to them the extent and seriousness of the cancer. When Dr. Andrews finally came out to talk to them, he was completely rattled and white as a ghost.

He had lost all semblance of his normal confident professionalism. He said that he had removed all of the cancer, but he could not stop the bleeding. He asked John if Jimmy had stopped his blood thinner as he had been directed to do before the surgery.

"I assume he did everything that he was told to do, doc." John replied.

As it turned out, that was not accurate at all. Not only that, Jimmy had failed to inform Dr. Andrews that he had been diagnosed with cirrhosis of the liver. Our family friend had almost expedited the death of our brother on the operating table because of details that Jimmy had not felt important enough to convey to his doctor, and a disregard for following instructions to the letter. Dr. Andrews was visibly shaken as he told the family that he would have never performed this surgery if he had known that he had been diagnosed with liver problems not to mention that he was still taking the blood thinner right up until yesterday.

Needless to say, Jimmy recovered from that, but that experience convinced me that someone had to pay closer attention to how he was taking his medications, how well he was eating, and just his general welfare.

Chapter Two

That Little Voice Inside

It took no time at all for us to get the motor home ready for the sixteen hour trip to Florida. Several hours into the trip, Jib called with an update from the doctor. The bleeding was caused by something called ascites. This is a common occurrence with a patient that has cirrhosis of the liver. Apparently, the esophagus becomes very thin like wet tissue paper and starts to bleed. Not one of us knew how serious this condition really was.

It was early evening when we finally arrived at the condo. Mike dropped me by the garage to pick up our vehicle, and I followed him over to the parking area where we stored the motorhome. He parked the motorhome, plugged in the electricity, locked the door, and we raced to the hospital. I hadn't heard anything else from Jib, so I assumed that everything was still calm. We went in through the emergency room door because the Intensive Care Unit was closer to that entrance. As we entered, I saw a familiar face behind the desk and I raced over to her asking where I could find my brother. She directed us to the area of the hospital set aside for those in serious condition.

The ICU rooms were enclosed in glass, so you could see into them even before we opened the door. As we reached his room, I could see him lying there with his eyes closed, but I could not tell if he was awake or asleep. Jib was sitting in a chair on the opposite side of his bed facing the open glass. She saw us as we walked up, and she stood up to meet us at the door. As we opened the door, he opened his eyes and just smiled at us.

"Boy, some people really know how to get attention," I joked as we walked in.

"I can't believe you guys got here so fast," was all he said as I leaned over and hugged him.

"I wanted to get here before you kicked the bucket," Mike kidded. We all laughed and breathed a sigh of relief as we saw that everything seemed to be ok at this point. Jimmy told us the same thing that Jib had told us on the phone, but when I quizzed him about what this all meant, he didn't seem to have any more knowledge than the rest of us.

"Did your doctor come by on his rounds this afternoon?" I asked.

"Oh yeah, he was here about 5:30 and he said that I am stabilized at this point."

"Well, why are they keeping you in ICU?" I quizzed him.

"I don't know...I didn't ask him that."

The four of us talked for a while and then Jib, who looked absolutely exhausted said, "I think I am going to go back to the house and take a shower and eat something. I have been here since 4:30 this morning and I am starving. All I've had today is junk out of the vending machines in the lobby.

"Jib, thank you so much for being here," I said.

She hugged Jimmy and we all said our good byes. I followed her out the door to see if she knew anything other than what Jimmy had told us. She insisted that Jimmy had told us everything that the doctor had told him. I hugged her and thanked her again for all that she had done for him and told her that we would see her in the morning.

As I walked back into the room, Mike and Jimmy were cracking jokes and kidding around like they always did with each other. You would never have guessed that an emergency had occurred less than sixteen hours ago if you hadn't realized that we were in the Intensive Care Unit in a hospital.

Finally, Jimmy insisted that we go home and get some rest. He assured us that he was alright now, and there was nothing we could do. We both hugged him and told him that we would be back bright and early tomorrow because we wanted to talk to his doctor. He just rolled his eyes and smiled. "Jayne, I'm a big boy."

"I know you are, but I just want to get it straight from your doctor if you don't mind!"

"You know that you are a pain in the…"

"Yes, and that's why you love me!" I laughed. "Get some rest and we will see you first thing in the morning," I said as I bent over and hugged him and kissed his cheek.

I looked back and smiled at him as Mike and I left his room, and he smiled and winked at me. As we walked down the hall, the dinner cart was being pushed into his room. Apparently, the doctor had decided that he was stable enough to finally eat something. If Jimmy had not had anything to eat all day, he was probably starving, so this would be a welcome sight for him.

Mike and I walked out of the hospital into the beautiful fall night in Florida. The temperature was perfect and the light sea breeze felt like a welcome kiss on our faces. I was exhausted, but so relieved that Jimmy was just fine, and he seemed like his usual 'happy go lucky' self. We decided that we would go by the motor home, get our cats, and collect a few things and go straight to the condo. We had plenty of food in the motor home, so we would just grab something from there for dinner. We would deal with everything else tomorrow after going to the hospital as early as possible, hopefully, catching Jimmy's doctor and finding out the specifics of this emergency.

Mike held my hand as we drove toward the motor home. "Are you ok?" he asked. "

Yes, I am now," I answered. "Thank you so much for being my rock. I don't know what I would do without you," I said as I kissed his hand.

We entered the motorhome knowing the tasks that each one of us would execute. We had done this so many times before it was almost an unconscious exercise. I crated the cats; Mike collected some food items and a few clothes. We packed it all into the car, locked the motor home, and headed to the condo. Everything seemed to be back to normal for now.

We pulled the car into the parking garage at the condo and started unloading things. We spoke to a few neighbors that were milling about on this beautiful evening, and handled our tasks at hand. When we were finally inside the condo with the door closed behind us, a feeling came over me that I have never experienced before. I have read accounts of panic attacks and out of body experiences, but those do not begin to describe the feeling that surged through my body. It was instantaneous like a bolt of lightning without the physical jolt. One second I was putting down fresh water for my cats and then the next second this surge went through me that filled my brain with one single thought...one single mission...I never heard a voice, but I knew that I had to get back to the hospital!

"Mike, I've got to go back to the hospital," I said trying to masque the terror I felt inside.

"What? Are you crazy? We just came from there! Jimmy's fine...he's probably asleep by now."

"I can't explain this," I choked as I started to feel the tears well up in my eyes. "You don't have to go; I just know that I've got to go back there!" I said, as I grabbed my purse and the keys to the car. He starred at me for a second and then I saw the look in his eyes that said, 'Ok, this is crazy, but count me in.'

We hurried back to the car with Mike jumping in on the driver's side. I will never be able to explain the feeling that had washed over me or why. I only knew that I HAD to go back to Jimmy's room! We were practically running down the hallway to his room in ICU just barely slowing down when we reached his doorway. He was lying there almost asleep it appeared, but I could tell that something was not quite right. He barely opened his eyes as Mike and I stood over him in the bed. His eyes did not seem to focus. He seemed disconnected or something. Then Mike asked him a question, and his response was garbled. Mike said to him, "Do you know who I am?"

He responded, "Mike, Mike, Mike…"

We looked at each other and both recognized that this was not right. I ran out of his room and to the nurses' station and asked if there was a doctor on the floor. The nurses couldn't understand why I was alarmed, so I explained that I didn't have time for a lot of chatter. I wanted a doctor in his room immediately! Finally, one of the nurses pointed to a doctor that was doing rounds in ICU. I quickly ran over to him, introduced myself, and explained what had just happened to my brother. He quickly followed me to

Jimmy's room, and proceeded to do a preliminary physical exam on him. He asked Jimmy, "Do you know where you are?" No response. Then he asked, "Do you know what day it is?"

Jimmy's response was completely incoherent. The doctor then pulled the sheet from the bottom of the bed and took Jimmy's foot in his hand. Using his pen, he scraped along the bottom of his foot and asked if he felt that. When Jimmy did not respond, he took a needle and stuck the bottom of his foot and his leg several times. Still there was no response at all from Jimmy. By this time, Jimmy's eyes were closed and he did not appear to be with us at all. The doctor explained to us that he may have had a stroke!

They asked that Mike and I wait down the hall in the waiting room while several doctors and nurses converged on Jimmy's room. As we walked to the waiting room, Mike held my hand and never said a word. He didn't have to. His eyes mirrored the terror I knew was in mine.

I have no idea how long we had been sitting there when the doctor came out to talk to us. He said that Jimmy had not had a stroke, but he was now in a coma.

I could only scream, "How can he be in a coma? We were just here with him earlier and he was fine! He was talking and laughing…just being himself. He thought his doctor was going to let him go home tomorrow."

This doctor tried to explain to us the chain of events that occurred after we left earlier in the evening. Apparently, when they delivered his dinner tray to him, the nurse insisted that he get out of bed, and sit in the chair to eat his meal. She helped him from the bed to the chair where he ate a little bit of his meal, and then she helped him back into the bed. Apparently, all that activity had caused his esophagus to start bleeding again. This blood was, of course, going into his stomach where a chemical reaction was occurring causing the incoherent speech and eventually the coma.

As it was already very late at night, the doctor told us to go on home because there was nothing that we could do tonight. He said that Jimmy's regular doctor would be there in the morning and he would be able to give us a more detailed report of his condition and what we could expect from here.

I reluctantly agreed to leave, but I wanted to see him before we left. This time when I entered the room, I was shocked by all the medical equipment hooked up to him. He looked so pale lying there. I couldn't hold back the tears as I took his hand in mine. I kissed it and told him, "I'll be back first thing in the morning and I expect you to be wide awake and ready to receive visitors." I knew in my heart that this would be the case, or at least it was what I hoped. Jimmy had pulled through much worse than this.

As we left the hospital for the second time that evening, I felt drained, confused, angry, and completely helpless. "How could this be?" I cried. "What just happened in there?" I practically screamed. Neither Mike nor I either one could wrap our minds around what we had just experienced. I could not stop the river of tears that just flooded from my eyes. "None of this makes any sense," I sobbed.

Chapter Three

In The Blink of an Eye

Mike just listened to me as we drove back to the condo. He was caught up in his own thoughts and could not offer me any comfort. "Jayne, you need to call Jib and let her know what is going on. She doesn't need to walk in there tomorrow morning and be faced with this without being prepared for it."

"You're right," I replied. "I guess I need to call Lee and John as well, don't you think?"

"Well, it's almost midnight now, so maybe you should wait until we talk to his doctor tomorrow morning before you get everybody all upset....plus, I think we need to get some sleep ourselves."

"I know you're right," I answered as I reached for my cell phone to call Jib. I hated to call her this late, but Mike was right. She did not need to walk into his room first thing tomorrow morning and see him like this without being prepared for it.

"Hello," Jib answered her phone.

"Jib, this is Jayne..."

"What's wrong, Jayne? It's after midnight. Is Jimmy ok?"

"No," I sobbed. "I'm afraid not!"

"Oh NO," she shouted. "What happened?"

Between sobs I told her all that had happened. I tried to explain to her how that strange feeling had washed over me that compelled me to return to the hospital even though we had just left there. "Mike must have thought I was crazy, but I am so glad that he went with me," I continued.

She, too, was distraught and confused. "He seemed fine when I left there this evening," she said.

"I know," was all I could say. "Even when we left there after you did, he was ok." I explained to her that he was now in a coma with a lot of equipment hooked up to him.

"Thank you for letting me know...I don't think I could manage if I had walked into his room in the morning and saw all those machines hooked up to him...." Her voice trailed off, and she was sobbing so hard it was difficult to understand her.

"Jib, try to get some sleep and we will see in the morning, ok? With that, we said our good byes and hung up.

As we pulled into the parking garage at the condo, I realized that we had not eaten anything since lunch time. No wonder I felt so weak and empty. Or was I empty because I knew that I was probably losing one of the basic foundations of my life...my big brother...my friend...my hero? At that thought, a river of sadness flooded over me that would probably never go away. The tears would eventually end, but I knew the sadness would linger for a lifetime.

So many things were running through my mind as we went inside. I had so many questions, and no answers. How could this be happening? Surely, this wasn't the end? He would be all right once his doctor got there in the morning and got things all straightened out, right? I felt so nauseated that I wanted to vomit, but there was nothing in me…nothing but a deep sadness that had consumed me. I just wanted the night to swallow me up and deliver me safely to the sunshine of a new day. A day that resembled nothing like this one. A day in which my 'big brother' greeted me with his usual smile and twinkle in his eye…full of life and laughter…and the promise of much more fun loving memories to share. This was not to be.

The alarm clock woke us at 6:00 a.m. We jumped out of bed, dressed quickly, grabbed a cup of coffee to take with us, and headed back to the hospital. We did not want to miss seeing his personal doctor that was supposed to be there by 7:00 a.m. When we arrived, Jib was already sitting there in a chair by his bed. Her eyes were swollen and red from the tears that were still flowing, and she looked like she had been there all night.

She stood up and met us at the door to his room. She hugged us both at the same time and sobbed as she said that Jimmy's doctor had been there since 5:00 a.m. He was already there when she arrived and he had looked over all the test results, and charts. He had run a couple of other tests himself and told her he would be back shortly. She said that was about 30 minutes ago, so she expected him back at any moment. All three of us just stood there looking at Jimmy's lifeless body as he lay there with all the machines and various beeping noises confirming to us that this was much more serious than we had expected. Not one of us made eye contact with the others because we knew that would start an avalanche of tears.

After what seemed an eternity, Jimmy's primary care doctor came into the room. The expression on his face told us all we needed to know. He came straight over to me and extended his hand as he said, "You must be Jim's sister?"

"Yes, I am," was all I could manage to say.

"I am Dr. Dominguez...so sorry that we have to meet under these conditions."

He must have noticed the tears welling up in my eyes as he introduced himself to Mike, acknowledged Jib, and then let out a deep sigh as he continued with his conversation. "We are in a very grave situation here," he said. "I'm afraid that it does not look very good for your brother. Do you mind if we step out into the waiting area?"

Everything that he said after that seemed to come from somewhere way off in the distance. It all felt so surreal...I was numb all over. If Mike had not put his arm around me, I think I would have collapsed on the floor.

Then I heard Mike speak as he asked Dr. Dominguez, "Are you saying that he may not come out of this coma?"

"Yes, I'm afraid that is the case here," he replied. "We are monitoring his brain activity now, and we are seeing a decrease in it hourly. In addition to the ascites, he seems to have suffered a stroke as well. We'll monitor his vitals to see if his organs start to shut down, but please know that even if we tried some heroic effort to stop the bleeding of his esophagus this would just be to do all over again in a day or so."

I could barely choke back the tears as I asked him, "What would you do if this were your brother?"

He took the stethoscope from around his neck, held it by his side, and looked me straight in the eyes. "I'm not speaking to you as a doctor now. I'm speaking as one compassionate human being to another. If this were my brother, I would let him go. I would not prolong his suffering by trying to save him…his esophagus is like wet tissue paper and there is nothing we can do that will ever change that…"

I buried my face in Mike's shoulder and muttered a thank you to the doctor. Dr. Dominguez shook our hands and said that he would keep us posted if there were any changes. He then expressed his sympathy as he turned and walked away.

The three of us went back into Jimmy's room without saying a word to each other. Mike was the first to speak. "I guess it's time to notify his kids, your other brothers…" His eyes filled with tears as he reached down for Jimmy's hand. He wanted to speak to Jimmy, but the words just wouldn't come out as he struggled to fight back the tears. The jokes and relaxed relationship that they had enjoyed for forty two years just melted away. The sadness in his eyes reflected what I was feeling in my heart.

Jib left the room crying. She just waved to us as she left as if to say, "I just can't handle this right now."

Taking Jimmy's other hand in mine, I kissed it gently and let the tears fall where they may. There are no words at a time like this that can ever describe the emotions you are feeling…no words console…no words take away the pain…every cell in your body feels raw. I have no idea how long Mike and I sat there like that listening to the gentle sounds of the equipment and the constant beep, beep, beep…Jimmy inhaling and exhaling.

Eventually, a nurse came in and fussed with the equipment and looked at Jimmy. All she said was, "Can I get you anything?"

We both just shook our heads and said, "No thanks."

"Mike, I guess it's time to make those phone calls, don't you?"

"Yes, I'm afraid so…do you know where his cell phone is?" he asked.

I opened the drawer in the table beside the bed and, of course, it was not there. "I'm sure it is still at his house."

"His phone has all the kids in it as well as all his Shriner buddies…his friends. We'll just divide the list up and start calling."

I stood up and kissed Jimmy on the forehead and said, "Jimmy, we'll be back shortly. We have to make some phone calls now…I love you very much…" I never knew that a heart could actually break into a thousand pieces until that moment.

Chapter Four

Shattered Hearts

Mike and I left the hospital and went by Jimmy's to pick up his phone. When Jib opened the door, we could see that she was still a mess. Her eyes were swollen and she looked like she hadn't slept in a week. I hugged her and told her how much I appreciated her being there for Jimmy and us. She offered to call some of the numbers in his phone, but we told her to just relax and try to get some sleep. We could handle this part. She informed us that she was going to go back up to the hospital and just sit there with him. She offered to fix lunch for us before she left, but we both passed on that idea. She had made plenty of fresh coffee which was gladly accepted.

I began by calling my brothers and sister. Everyone was in total shock. Lee and John planned to be there right away, but the other two, the twins, could not make it. I even called Jimmy's ex-wife, Toni. She was equally shocked and devastated by the news. Jimmy and Toni had been divorced for about ten years, but she was still like a sister to me. She decided that she should call her two children, Jim and Sabrina, and Jimmy's oldest daughter from a previous marriage. We agreed with that decision. It took several hours to reach everyone that needed to be notified, but then the phones started ringing and they wouldn't stop. I guess the news was growing exponentially. People were calling his cell phone from all over the country trying to verify the awful news. Mike and I decided that we had better keep his phone with us and try to handle all the queries.

We soon realized that we had planes to meet, accommodations to provide for family members, and so many questions to answer. In the blink of an eye, this went from a private loss and tragedy to an out of control frenzy. I just wanted to be alone in my grief...alone by my brother's side. I had so much I needed to say to him...so much he needed to know before he left me.

The next couple of days were just a blur. I can't remember if we even ate or slept during that time, but I do remember the afternoon that Dr. Dominguez pulled me aside in the hospital and told me that my brother was brain dead. He said that he should be moved from the ICU to hospice care now. Even though I knew this day was coming, I was still devastated when it actually arrived. The doctor told me that they would try to keep him as comfortable as possible, but no medical care would be provided there. With a heavy heart, I made the appropriate arrangements and informed the family.

Before the ambulance service arrived to move him from the hospital to the hospice care facility, I asked to be alone with Jimmy. Mike herded everyone out of the room and closed the door behind him. I closed the blinds on the glass wall that ran the length of the hallway outside his room. I had no way of knowing if he could hear me or not, but I decided this was my last chance to pour my heart out to my 'big brother,' my friend, my hero.

I sat down on the side of his bed, took his hand in mine, kissed it gently as the tears started to flow freely again, and said, "Oh Jimmy... I am so sorry for the decisions I've had to make here...I wish you could tell me what to do...I wish I could just know what you are thinking right now...I don't know what I'm going to do without my big brother...you have always been there for me...I would ask you not to leave, but that would be selfish...I don't want you to suffer anymore." I continued with tears streaming down my cheeks, "I will handle everything the way you wanted it done...even the funeral...you prepared me well. You told me you were going to die at age 72...I didn't want to believe you....Jimmy, I don't think I've ever said thank you for all that you did for me as a child. My life would have been such a mess if you hadn't been there for me...you helped me see that there was so much more to life...you made me reach higher...you protected me when I wasn't able to take care of myself...thank you for sharing your deepest darkest secrets with me…I hope you know that you could never say or do anything that could ever make me love you less…you will always be my hero…you will always be in my heart…and I will always love my 'big brother'," I sobbed.

There was a knock on the door. The ambulance service was there to take him to the hospice facility. I kissed his hand one last time and gently laid it beside his body. This was final proof that there was no turning back from here. My 'big brother' was going to cease to exist.

I signed the paper work and Mike and I left before the ambulance did. We went straight over to the hospice facility…the very same hospice that Jimmy had donated so much to in past years. We entered the front door and were met by volunteers that had already been alerted that we were on our way and so was Jimmy. There was more paper work to sign and a quick tour of the facility. About that time, the ambulance arrived with Jimmy on a stretcher. They brought him in and set him up in his room. At least here he wasn't hooked up to all those machines. There was a small CD player in his room playing very soothing, soft music. I couldn't help but think that Jimmy would have preferred George Jones, Tammy Wynette, or Conway Twitty to that 'elevator music.'

One by one, family members started straggling in. Lee and John, our two brothers, Jim and Sabrina, two of his children, Jib, and of course, the two of us were all packed into his little room. Then there were the ever ringing cell phones. I had reached a point that I could not take any more calls on Jimmy's cell phone. Mike had taken over that job completely. I was thankful that he would step out of hearing distance every time he had to take one of those calls to update one of Jimmy's friends or worse yet, inform someone that had just heard the news.

There was one phone call that shattered my already broken heart. This call came on Sabrina's cell phone. It was her mother, Toni, calling to see how Sabrina was doing. She was doing about as poorly as you would expect a loving daughter to be doing at this point, but she kept her vigil right there by Jimmy's side. At one point in her conversation, her mother must have asked her to put the phone to Jimmy's ear because she did so without hesitation or question. None of us in the room could hear what was being said, but the tears were just pouring from Sabrina's eyes as her parents...her mother was saying her goodbye to the love of her life...the father of her children. Regardless of the divorce that occurred ten years ago, everyone in that room knew that Toni still loved him.

I had to leave the room. The beautiful fall day outside belied the fact that our world was crumbling beneath our feet. Nothing would ever be the same. I found my way to the memory garden. It was such a peaceful, soothing place. I sat down on a bench and just let more tears flow. My cell phone rang. On the other end of my phone was someone who wanted to see if Jimmy could get their grandbaby into the Shriner's Children's Hospital. I didn't know whether to laugh or cry! Here my brother was on his death bed, literally, and someone wanted a favor from him. After explaining the situation to them, I assured the person on the other end that I would be seeing his Shriner brothers at the funeral and I would have them contact her. One of them would be happy to sponsor this child. After all, that's what they did. Jimmy would have if only he could.

The next couple of days were filled with so many people coming to say good bye to my brother. There was sadness in the air that seemed to smother each of us at times. Mike and I did not leave his side unless we had to because we knew that the end was close. The attendants told us that his organs were starting to shut down and he probably would not last very much longer. There were so many of us packed into his little room waiting for his last breath. Lee even made the comment that Jimmy would never leave while there was a party going on. How true that was! Jimmy was always the life of the party…but this was a gathering that I would have given anything to cancel. Then it happened. There was no dramatic fanfare…no earth shattering moment that signaled the end of a beautiful life…the end of someone that had been so loved and depended upon…he merely inhaled for the last time then exhaled for an extremely long sigh…then he was gone! November 8, 2008 an otherwise beautiful fall day. He had turned seventy two years old on February 27, 2008.

Everyone in the room just held hands and started weeping. The expression on the faces in the room portrayed such sadness that it will forever be written on my heart. Finally, they started exiting the room, and Mike and I were left there alone with him. I leaned over and kissed his forehead and said, "I love you, 'Big Brother.' You are going to be missed very much. Thank you again for always being there for me."

My brother told me many times how he wanted his funeral and burial to be done. I lovingly appeased him never dreaming that I would actually have to use that information one day. He wanted a military graveside service with the Mason's conducting their customary service for one of their own. He was to be buried in our hometown cemetery where our sister, Faye, was buried beside our Aunt Mary and Uncle Monk. This last request required his body to be flown from Florida to the Atlanta airport and then transported by hearse to the small town outside of Atlanta for burial.

Before that could be accomplished, I had to go to his home and select the suit, tie, and other garments that he would be buried in. Mike and I unlocked the front door of Jimmy's house and entered into a place that was devoid of life now. It felt like all the life had been sucked out of this once cozy, comfortable, welcoming home. I found my way to his walk-in closet, and with Mike's help, we selected everything that would be needed for the burial. I felt like a robot going through a series of preprogramed actions.

We took the garments to the funeral home where Jimmy's body had been taken after his death. Thankfully, my brothers, John and Lee, helped me select the coffin, but I still could not shake the numbness that I felt in my heart.

Because of the number of people that were unable to travel to Florida to see him before he died, I decided that I would have a 'viewing' at the local funeral home in our hometown prior to the interment. That was the only decision unilaterally made.

Long before his death, he had established a website to accomplish his goal for 2010 of raising a total of one million dollars to contribute to the Shriner's Children Hospital, so we requested that instead of flowers, the family would be most grateful if they would make a contribution to his lifelong charity organization. His Shriner Lodge handled all of that.

After all the arrangements were made on both ends, Mike and I decided to take our motorhome to Georgia for the burial. We could spend a few days there before and after the ceremony and tie up any loose ends that may exist there. I honestly do not remember much about the trip up there or the events leading up to the burial. I just remember being consoled by so many people from my childhood that had known my brother for a lifetime. People came from all over the country; some that had worked with him during his career with General Motors; others were just neighbors at one time or another. There was even a young family there that remembered their children calling him 'Poppa Jim' because he was their surrogate grandfather. They had even brought handmade cards that they wanted to put in his coffin with him so he would always remember them. He would have been so pleased to see the outpouring of love from so many people. I know I was.

Since there was no pastor, priest, or any other religious person to conduct the service (per Jimmy's request), the funeral director asked if we wanted to share thoughts or comments after the military and Mason's finished their part of the ceremony. We decided that it might be a good idea to let anyone that wanted to share a story about Jimmy, do so at that time. Then, I would finish by thanking everyone for being there.

The viewing at the funeral home lasted for about two hours. There were so many people there. Jimmy's coffin was open the entire time and everyone just visited and talked to each other. Some of them had not seen each other for years, while others, were involved in each other's daily lives. There were pictures of Jimmy from childhood all the way through his most recent Shriner picture decked out in his fez and tuxedo.

It was a short distance from the funeral home to the cemetery, but there was still a long processional following the hearse. His coffin was draped with an

American Flag and soldiers stood guard by his gravesite. Military funerals always tug at my heart strings, but this one was especially difficult. The folding and presenting of the flag to the family and the playing of 'taps,' left not one dry eye in the group. The Masons did their part honoring one of their own, a 33rd degree Mason, and it was very emotional as well. What an honorable and worthy organization of brothers. Jimmy would have been so pleased.

The funeral director then asked if anyone would like to say a few words or share a story with the group. After a slight hesitation, people started coming forward expressing funny, inspiring, and uplifting stories. Jimmy's children enjoyed hearing all of this, but they were unable to participate because they were sobbing so hard. My brothers each said a few words and told how they would miss him and what an impact he had on their lives. Mike shared a treasured memory of Jimmy. Then it was my turn.

I just remember looking out over the crowd as I stood by my brother's coffin and thinking to myself; every one of these people shared an active role in his life, and they, too, were all going to miss him and the joy and laughter he brought to their world.

I began by saying, "If you knew my brother well, you know he wasn't perfect," I fought hard to hold back the tears as I continued… "But if you looked past that imperfection, you saw a man with a heart of gold. He was never able to ignore anyone that was in pain or suffering in any way. He was always the first one on the scene to give a hand or provide assistance that was needed. He was always the first to help provide for those that were less fortunate. Each of you played a major role in his life…I know he loved all of you…He made a huge difference in my life, and I know there is a hole in my heart that will never be filled….When you think of him, always remember his smile and the mischief that was always present in his eyes….My family and I thank all of you for coming today…We are so grateful for such outpouring of love and respect…I know that Jimmy would be so pleased."

Then, following the instructions that Jimmy had insisted that I do after his burial, I invited anyone that was able to attend to join us at his favorite seafood restaurant there in town. His exact words had been, "I don't want people to be sad when I'm gone…I want you to have one last party on me!" So we did!

Chapter Five

The Visit

It had only been a week since we returned from the graveside service in Georgia, but my emotions were still quite raw. I could just think of him, or pass by the street where he lived, or think of something he had said and I would cry for hours. I thought losing my mother was difficult, but for some reason, I was better prepared to lose her than I was to lose my sibling, my big brother. I don't know how our brains process grief, but I do know that it comes in waves. Sometimes the grief would completely paralyze me and at other times it was just a nagging sadness that wouldn't go away.

I tried to keep myself busy with preparations for Thanksgiving. Our entire family had decided that we would all be together for this holiday because Jimmy had been looking so forward to it. We now understood that he knew this would be his last, if he could make it that far. We decided to make this a celebration of his life and go ahead with the plans as he had made them. The only difference being that we would not have it at his house, and of course, he would not be there.

That night I went to bed at my usual time with nothing out of the ordinary on my mind. I found that sleep was a welcome relief from the grief, so I welcomed it gladly. I don't know how long I had been asleep when my eyes instantly flew open as if I had been awakened by a sudden noise or intruder. I looked at my bedside clock and saw that it was exactly 4:00 a.m. My husband was sound asleep next to me quietly inhaling and exhaling. My room was completely dark except for the light from the digital clock. I lay there with my eyes wide open trying to figure out what had so abruptly awakened me. Then I saw him.

He was coming toward me escorted on each side by two figures that were holding his arms as if to give him support. They were not walking, but floating. The two figures assisting him looked somewhat like people without any distinguishable features at all. They were almost as dark as the darkness of my room, so they appeared to be three dimensional shadows. They were much smaller than my brother who was six feet tall, so I assumed that they were females. I jumped out of bed and went to greet him. As he moved closer to me, the two figures just melted into the darkness of my bedroom, and Jimmy was left standing there alone in front of me. I knew I wasn't dreaming. I was completely awake and standing in front of him!

I was so happy to see him, but I could not stop the gush of tears that were streaming down my face. Somehow, I knew not to touch him even though I wanted to hug him so badly. I just stood there face to face with him and immediately started firing questions at him. I asked, "How was your journey?" That question sounded odd even to me.

He slowly with great effort replied, "Difficult… and…. confusing."

I could tell that he was still very weak and sickly, but the oddest thing was happening as I questioned him. He would fade from the sick, death bed image at the Hospice to the young handsome man that I remembered as a child. This was very unsettling to me at first, and it took a few minutes for me to figure out what was happening. I think he had not yet received his new, healthy body that some believe we will have when we go to heaven. I asked him how he was able to come to me and he said, "I don't really know…I was sent back here to give you a message…I don't have much time, so…"

I interrupted him and blurted out, "I am so sorry for the decision I had to make there in the hospital. I have second guessed myself every day since then. I didn't want to let you go, but the doctor told me that this would just be to do over again in a few days or weeks. You could not recover from this…" I sobbed as I realized that we were not actually speaking words to each other. It was as if we were hearing each other's thoughts.

"I know...I heard him too. You did what I wanted you to do. I heard all of you talking as you stood by my bed... Lee was right... I didn't want to leave you... It was the hardest thing I ever had to do."

I don't know what made me say this, but I asked, "Have you seen God yet?"
That was a strange question for me to ask because God had not been part of my life in a very long time. I don't think I even believed in Him anymore.

He answered, "Whew... yes and it was... very... trying."

Needless to say, this really shook me up. "What did He say?" I almost gasped.

"He said that I have a lot of work to do."

I held my breath as I asked my next question. "What does He look like?"

"He is beautiful...almost blinding...words can't describe Him."

I could see that he was so weak and without the assistance of the other two beings, it was a struggle for him to keep talking to me, but he went on. "Jayne, we were wrong...I was sent back here to tell you...that you have got to change your heart and mind so you don't end up in this position."

"Jimmy, you are scaring me," I said. "What kind of work do you have to do and how long is it going to take you?"

"I can't go in to that...I just know I have to make amends for a lot of things that I've done. I have no idea how long it will take.... I thought doing good things would be enough..."

"Who sent you back here?" I asked with my voice quivering.

"God..." was all he could manage to answer.

All I could do was cry as I listened to him continue. "Tell Toni that I am sorry...she deserved so much better than me...I know she loved me, but I did so many wrong things to her...I heard what she said on the phone, and I wanted to tell her that she had been a good wife...that I love her for putting up with me...thank her for her prayers...but I couldn't get it out. Please make sure that she knows."

"Jimmy, I never thanked you for all the wonderful things you did for me my whole life. I don't know what I would have done or how my life would have turned out if you hadn't been my big brother," I sobbed.

"I know...I heard you in the hospital...I know you have always appreciated the things I did, and I know you have always loved me...that's why I have to make you understand...that's why I'm here. The devil is like a roaring lion prowling the earth looking for unsuspecting, weak people to devour. Where you are now is just temporary...just a dream...If you turn your back on Jesus, He will turn his back on you."

I couldn't stop the tears from flowing and I could hardly talk myself. I just kept watching him fade from sickly to healthy and young with a million questions flying around inside my head. I really wanted to touch him and hug him one last time, but I knew I couldn't.

"Our Mother was right about God and all the things that she tried to teach us. You have got to go back to the things we learned as kids...she was right.

God is real and we do have to pay for our sins...You've got to ask for forgiveness for your sins and ask Jesus to come into your heart and save you if you want to spend eternity in heaven... He's the only way," he continued. "Please tell everyone that I'm ok... and don't worry about me. I will do the work God wants done, but I don't want you to go through this."

"Will you be able to come back to me and let me know how you are doing?" I asked. "Will I know if you get all your work done?"

He gave me a little smile and answered, "I will try."

"No, please promise me that you will come back and let me know that you are all right!" As the tears continued to flood my face, I was very conscious of the fact that neither one of us uttered a sound. Not even my crying and sobbing was audible. I felt like I was in another dimension or some kind of void where time or space didn't exist, but I was right there in my own bedroom. How could Mike, who is a very light sleeper, not wake up and see this miraculous exchange between two worlds taking place?

"If I can, I will....I promise...You have to accept God and believe everything that we were taught...You have to ask Jesus to come into your heart...He is the only way...There are things that you can't possibly understand now..." Before he could continue I saw his two escorts return to each side of him, and I knew his time with me was over. I looked at my clock and it was exactly 5:00 a.m. He had been there with me exactly sixty minutes. "Jimmy, I love you very much and I miss you so much I can't stand it."

"I love you, too, Sis... I'll always be your big brother," he said as they turned and melted into the darkness of my room. They floated right out of sight through the same area of darkness that they had entered into my room.

By this time, I was crying hysterically, and I realized that I had forgotten to ask him if he had seen our Mother, our sister, Faye, our Grandparents, or our Dad. I called out to him, "Wait, I just want to ask you one more question... wait, don't go," but he was gone. I just collapsed on the floor, crying from a pain so deep inside that it is indescribable.

My yelling must have finally awakened Mike because he started calling out to me and trying to find me. "Jayne, where are you? What's wrong? Are you ok?"

I couldn't speak. I was crying so hard that I couldn't breathe. He finally found me in a fetal position on the floor. He knelt down pulling me close to him probably thinking that I had finally had some kind of mental break down. I just kept sobbing and trying to breathe. I finally told him what had happened and about the conversation I had just had with my brother. I tried desperately to remember everything that Jimmy had told me. Somehow, I knew that he had made a great sacrifice to come to me and warn me. I didn't want to ever forget a single word of his message.

Later that day, after I collected myself, I went to my computer and wrote down every word that I could remember, but I couldn't shake the feeling that I was not remembering all of it. I knew that this was the most important event of my life, and it had to be some kind of miracle. I was afraid to talk to anyone but Mike about this because I knew they would think I was crazy.

Occasionally, I would reread every word that I had written down, second guessing every question that I had asked him. I could think of so many questions that I should have asked, and I wished that I had not interrupted him and just let him do the talking, but how can anyone ever be prepared for such an event? I had to stop beating myself up and just accept the fact that I had blown the interview opportunity of a lifetime.

Chapter Six

Celebrate Life

Our family did have that Thanksgiving that Jimmy wanted so badly to have. Everyone was there including his Great Grandson who was only three years old. Even his ex-wife, Toni, who had divorced him ten years earlier, was there and she was welcomed as a sister. I hoped he was there in spirit and loving every minute of it. Why wouldn't he be? After the experience I had, I no longer doubted any possibility.

We took turns telling our favorite 'big brother' experiences which caused everyone to laugh so hard that we had tears running down our cheeks. He surely laughed more than any of us.

Toni and I shared one of our funniest memories of Jimmy when we had taken a vacation together just the four of us. We were at a first class resort in Florida sitting poolside with our deck chairs lined up one by one just working on our tans and reading when all of a sudden a flock of sea gulls flew over with their noisy chatter. We had all seen that before, so that was not a big deal. However, not one of us was prepared for what happened next. All of a sudden we heard plop, splat, plop…then this unbelievable string of expletives from Jimmy as he realized that one or more of those birds had decided to poop on him as they flew over! He was the only one that was hit! Needless to say, he was furious, but the rest of us could not stop laughing for hours! It took him a long time to live down his visit from the 'bird of paradise.'

One of my favorite stories was about an old girlfriend named Sandra, who was like a big sister to me when I was a kid. She taught me how to 'jitter bug,' how to wear lipstick, and how to be a girl in general which was a task because I had three older brothers and one younger. She was beautiful as a young girl, but when Jimmy hooked up with her again, she was almost seventy with Grandchildren of her own. He didn't seem to care though. She was still beautiful to him.

He took her to Paris on vacation one year and that turned out to be the most hilarious vacation ever! He had told how they landed in Paris where he rented a car at the airport so they could go sightseeing on their own. He hadn't realized it at the time, but it takes a very savvy driver to maneuver around Paris, and since he had maneuvered the back roads of Georgia, he knew he could handle Paris! However, parking would turn out to be even more of a challenge. Anyway, he picked up his rental car at the airport in Paris and proceeded to drive to the hotel where they had reservations. He could see the name of the hotel on the side of the building high up in the air, but he just couldn't get to it. After driving for what must have been hours, he could not get any closer to the hotel. He finally parked the car and announced his decision to Sandra. The shortest way to get from point A to point B is 'as the crow flies,' and since he couldn't drive it, he would walk it. He told Sandra, "The hotel is just over there a few blocks. You stay here and I will be back as soon as I register us and find someone that can tell me where to park."

Sandra reluctantly agreed and said, "Ok, but don't be long! Remember I don't speak French!"

He assured her that he would only be a few minutes and he took off on foot. After walking around in circles for an hour or so, he finally arrived at the hotel. He walked into the lobby and registered. Unfortunately, the hotel did not have parking accommodations which was pretty normal for Paris, but not Georgia! After a minute or two of *"You have got to be kidding me!"* he decided he would look around for somewhere to park anyway.

It was now very late afternoon and the sun was slowly setting in the sky. He was worried about Sandra being mad at him for taking so long, so he decided he had better get back to the car, so he started trying to retrace his steps. Remember, it had been hours since he left Sandra, the luggage, and the car. He walked and walked; the more he walked the darker it got. He went up one street and down another, but he could not find where he left her. He thought to himself, *'this sure ain't like Georgia! I better get some help!'* Finally, he saw a Paris Police Officer, so with his thick southern accent he asked the officer, "Sir, can you help me find my car and my girlfriend? I parked my car with my girlfriend and luggage in it and walked over to the hotel because I couldn't find anywhere close to the hotel to park, but now I can't find my way back." He was pleasantly surprised to find that the officer could speak English and understood all that he had said.

The officer looked at him fighting hard to keep from laughing and asked, "On what street did you park your car?"

"Uh, I don't know," he replied as he removed his hat and scratched his head.

The police officer looked at his partner and tried to hold back his laughter but failed. When he finished laughing, he said, "I cannot help you find your car, your girlfriend, or your luggage if you cannot remember on what street you parked, but you must remember you are in Paris! You can walk everywhere; you can buy clothes everywhere; and best of all, Paris is known for its beautiful women, so lucky for you, you can always find another girlfriend!" As they drove off laughing, he chuckled, "have fun in Paris!

Jimmy kept walking and eventually found the car and Sandra. She was furious to say the least because she thought he had left her there on purpose! Needless to say, I don't think the romantic trip to Paris turned out quite like he had planned, but we sure did have fun laughing about his Paris vacation.

Mike told the story about the day that he, Jimmy, and I went for a boat ride in Jimmy's super-fast ski boat. Jimmy had just brought his newly renovated ski boat down from Georgia and he needed to take it on a test run. We put it in the water at the condo boat ramp and took off. Mike drove while Jimmy and I sat on the back deck with our feet resting on the seats. There was nothing to hold on to, but we didn't consider that to be a problem. We were just cruising around in the Gulf channel enjoying the perfect Florida day.

Just as we were about to enter the no-wake area, a huge Casino shuttle boat was coming out of the no-wake zone. The shuttle boat carrying about 300 people powered up and took off. The boat turned right in front of us causing a huge wake 4-5 feet high. We were still traveling at a good rate of speed, so we hit the wave hard. We hit it so hard that it knocked Mike out of the driver's seat, but somehow he managed to hang onto the steering wheel. Jimmy and I didn't fare as well.

I saw that we were about to hit the wake from the shuttle hard, so I grabbed for the only thing that I could which was a rope secured to something in the boat, and at the same time, I grabbed for Jimmy to help keep him in the boat. Unfortunately, as I reached for him, all I grabbed was his hat because he was already headed overboard. I screamed at the top of my lungs, "Jimmy's overboard!"

Once we cleared that initial wave, the others weren't so bad, so Mike was quickly able to gain control of the boat. He turned around and saw the terrified look on my face and Jimmy's hat in my hand.

A man overboard was bad enough, but to add to the stress, there were boats everywhere. All we could think about was Jimmy getting hit by one of those boats or getting knocked unconscious when he went overboard. Either way, I was panicked! Mike circled the boat back around to look for Jimmy. We searched frantically for him, but all we could see were crab traps with their typical white foam ball about 10 inches in diameter bobbing in the water everywhere. Then I saw one about a hundred yards behind us bobbing up and down differently from all of the other ones. We thought that must be him, so we turned around and headed that way. Mike started laughing uncontrollably. I guess he was relieved to see that he was all right, but I didn't see it that way at all. It just looked to me like his head bobbing in the water. I screamed at Mike, "He's been decapitated!"

As we approached him, Mike started yelling to Jimmy over and over, "Are you OK?" Jimmy gave no response confirming my fear of decapitation. Then Mike gave the thumbs up sign hoping that Jimmy would respond with his thumb up in the air to let us know that he was all in one piece. Still, Jimmy gave no response. Finally, we got close enough for Jimmy to hear Mike asking if he was ok. That was the best 'thumbs up' I have ever seen! Now, we both started laughing and could not stop. After we got him in the boat, Mike asked him why he hadn't given a 'thumbs up' sooner. He explained that he had lost his glasses when he went overboard and couldn't see anything. It took Jimmy a while to see the humor in this, but eventually, we were all laughing.

    As everyone took their turn telling their favorite story about their 'big brother,' Dad, Grandpa, or great friend, I just sat back and watched their faces and how their sorrow was turned to happiness as they remembered their time spent with Jimmy and all the memories they shared with him. He had meant so much to all of us. Even the youngest members of the family shared their stories. He loved them all so much and was famous for his jokes and pranks he would play on them. He was often referred to as the 'jokester' by many of them because he could be relentless. We were also reminded of his generosity when the little ones talked about surprise presents like bikes, or scooters, or games that he would find and present to them for no reason at all except that he just loved them. He never missed one of my Grandchildren's birthday parties. As a matter of fact, he attended several that we were unable to attend because we were so far away in the motor home. Somehow, I know we were not missed at all because 'Uncle Jimmy' was there!

Although his sense of humor was legendary, you couldn't talk about Jimmy without bringing up his generous nature. He was a 33rd degree Mason and a Shriner who spent his entire adult life raising money for the Shriner's Children's Hospital. After he retired, he worked every fall for weeks at the Shriner's Circus in Marietta, Georgia raising money for the hospital. He was also a 'road warrior' for the Shriner's. That was a person that would drive a sick child and their family to whatever Shriner's Children's Hospital deemed best suited for their treatment. Sometimes this was several states away from where they lived. He would stay with the family as long as they needed him and sometimes he would drive them back home when the child was discharged from the hospital. He did all that using his own resources. He also spent hours transporting wounded or elderly veterans to the VA Hospital in Tampa and waiting for them to finish their appointments then driving them back home.

Of course, my siblings and I had to remind everyone how generous Jimmy had been to us as children. Each one of us recalled an incident that warmed our hearts as we remembered how much he had contributed to our lives. I told them about the shiny new saxophone Jimmy purchased for me when I went into the fourth grade. He could have rented one or purchased a used one, but he made sure that I had a new one, and he paid for all the lessons all the way through high school. That saxophone turned out to be an extension of my identity because I played in the junior high band and the high school band. I competed in state competitions every year and won several state awards over the years. Jimmy even paid for baton twirling lessons and camps that I attended each summer. Because of that, I went on to become a majorette in both junior high and high school. I could never have enjoyed any of those privileges if he had not been the generous 'big brother' that he was.

I wanted so badly to tell them about his visit with me, but I just couldn't bring myself to talk about it. They wouldn't understand any way or worse yet, they would think I had lost my mind. I was also conflicted and worried about what he said about 'the work he had to do.' I decided that this was not the right time to bring that up. I needed to figure this out before I burdened anyone else with this.

Chapter Seven

Grief and Memories

Jimmy loved all the holidays, but Thanksgiving was his favorite. He would always plan great elaborate family get-togethers or travel events that centered around that holiday. Thanksgiving 2004 was one that I will always remember. Before our Mother passed away in 1998, Jimmy had always wanted to have a family reunion that would have been just for her. Due to circumstances beyond his control and the divorce that he was going through at that time, he just never managed to get it all planned. Then when our Mother passed away, he suffered from extreme guilt even though she never knew what he was planning or ever expected such an elaborate event.

In 2004, to mitigate his guilt, Jimmy planned and coordinated a week long 'family reunion' cruise. Most of our siblings and their spouses attended along with my Mother's sister and her husband. My Aunt Alice and Uncle Richard were getting quite elderly by this time, and they had never been on a cruise before, so Jimmy decided it would be a great idea if we could all be together for seven days and share this great family time with them. The cruise was a great idea because no one would have to cook or clean or worry about any of the details involved in hosting and planning a family reunion. It was the most fun we ever had as a family.

We cruised all through the Caribbean stopping at several islands along the way. The weather was perfect and the food was fabulous. Because my family is famous for our competitive Scrabble games, we decided while we were on this cruise that we would hold the 'International Scrabble Tournament' and settle once and for all who the best Scrabble player really was in the family. The social director on the cruise found us a private 'gambling' room right off the casino aboard ship, and we used that room for our elimination matches. The tournament literally went on for seven full days. In order to be eligible for the championship round which was only four players, each player had to win so many games. Needless to say, it was not long before we had other passengers on the cruise begging to get in on our game. We had to explain to them that this was a private 'grudge' match that was going to settle who the Scrabble champion was in our family.

All of us including my elderly aunt played until we eliminated all but the last four players that would compete in the final round. I am proud to say that I had a seat at that table as did my husband, Mike, and my brothers, John and Bill. There were so many people packed into that little room to see who was going to take home that coveted title of 'International Scrabble Champion' that it was actually uncomfortable. I regret to say that my husband beat us all and I came in second! We became known as the 'Scrabble family' aboard ship.

My Aunt and Uncle had never been out of the United States, so it was quite a thrill for them to visit all the little islands in the Caribbean. Jimmy delighted in ushering them around and seeing their reactions to all the different sights and cultures on these islands. He bought them all kinds of souvenirs and had so many pictures made of them both on and off ship. I didn't realize it at the time, but in a way, Jimmy was doing this for our Mother. I could see in his eyes how much he missed our Mother and how he regretted that he had not been able to do this for her.

One of my favorite times of the cruise occurred every evening at dinner time when we all gathered around the huge table they prepared just for us, and enjoyed being together laughing and telling stories about the events of the day. Jimmy wore his unofficial title of 'family patriarch' very well.

In 2006, he planned another cruise with his children Jim, Sabrina, and Phyllis and their spouses. I don't know how or why I was included in that event, but I will always be grateful for that wonderful memory. In retrospect, I now realize that Jimmy was saying goodbye to all of us.

Of course, the cruise was a happy, joyous experience. We danced, sang karaoke, explored islands, and just about everything imaginable, but I did notice that Jimmy wasn't quite his exuberant self. Several evenings he retired early to his cabin and he had very little alcohol to drink. At the time, we were all having so much fun that no one even noticed or commented on it. Oh how I wish I could have known then what was really going on.

Chapter Eight

Financial Tragedy

In the days and weeks that passed after his death, I spent a lot of time alone walking on the beach, sitting alone on the beach, or just quietly trying to be invisible. I knew I was grieving, very depressed, and completely confused. Christmas was just around the corner which was always a joyous family time for us, but I just couldn't get myself motivated to make any plans, do any decorating, or do any Christmas shopping at all. Honestly, I just wanted to be left alone in my grief and confusion. Truth be known, what I really wanted was my brother back. What I really wanted was not to have this burden on my heart that was beginning to consume me.

I wished that I could just brush his visit off as a silly dream or the result of a brain that was overloaded and malfunctioning, but in my heart, I knew I couldn't. I knew that my brother had returned to give me a message from a God that I didn't even really believe in. Was he correct when he said, "that you have to go back to what we learned as kids…our mother was right…there is a God and we have to pay for our sins?"

I was even more confused by, "God said I have a lot of work to do." I am definitely no Biblical scholar, but I don't ever remember anyone saying that we have an opportunity to make up for our sins after we die. The more I questioned that statement, the more confused I became.

In addition, I must admit that every single night that I went to bed I hoped that Jimmy would return to let me know that he had done whatever it was that God said he had to do. He didn't exactly promise me that he would, but he did promise that he would try. All my life as a child and an adult, he always delivered on his promises. I began to think that maybe I was walking that fine line between sanity and insanity.

Just when I thought that life could not get any more difficult or sad, Mike received a phone call from his boss in Houston. It just happened to be Mike's sixty third birthday, December 15th, so he thought it was just an obligatory birthday wish. He answered his cell phone cheerfully, but as I watched, his countenance went from jovial to almost angry. He finished his conversation, closed his phone, and sat down on the sofa. He looked like the blood had drained from his head. Then he said, "They just laid me off. My boss just said, *don't bother to return to Houston until further notice.*"

I plopped down beside him and blinked back tears, "For how long?" I questioned.

"He didn't say. He only said that he was laying off over one hundred people…production has screeched to a halt, sales have plummeted since the election, orders have been cancelled, and there seems to be nothing positive in sight."

"What in the world are we going to do?" I cried. We had a little savings, and some things we could cut back on, so Mike assured me that we would be able to weather this storm. Boy did that turn out to be a gross miscalculation.

Looking back, I don't know how we managed to get through that Christmas because the economic news just kept getting worse and worse. Florida seemed to dive head first into the worst economic recession our country had seen in decades. So many people we knew lost their jobs, their homes, their businesses, and the rest of the country seemed to follow suit. We saw condos in our community that senior citizens just walked away from because they lost their retirement investments in the stock market and could no longer afford to pay the maintenance fees, taxes, or utilities. Most of them were being forced to move back up north to live with their children or grandchildren. At one point, the statistics showed that a staggering number, approximately eight thousand people, were leaving Florida daily! We even heard of a retired surgeon that had taken a job as a security guard in his condo community and his wife was baking at Publix to make ends meet. They lost millions in their retirement investment program. Sadly, this was not an isolated incident.

It didn't take Mike long to realize that he was not going to be called back to work. He was going to have to find something quickly or we were going to join the ranks of those that were losing everything. He made phone calls daily touching base with people nationwide that he knew. Everyone seemed to be of the same mind set. No one was hiring. In fact, most were trimming their employees as well. Things really looked bleak for us.

I began to focus on the message that Jimmy gave me. God seemed to be working really hard to get my attention. What more did He need to do to wake me up and pull me out of my forty year 'spiritual desert?'

I was more than a little fearful at this point. This God that could send my brother back here with a message for me could obviously do anything that He chose to do! After all, He merely spoke the words and the entire universe was created in six days! (*Genesis 1:*

1-25) What if He was so angry with me that He just decided to vaporize me like the 'Star Trek' characters that were shot with those make believe weapons! Yes, I knew He was capable of anything because I remembered stories from my childhood of the God of the Old Testament that wiped out entire cities with no effort at all. *"Thus he overthrew those cities and the entire plain, including all those living in the cities—and also the vegetation in the land. (Genesis 19: 25)* or flooded the whole world to get rid of sinners that He thought could not be redeemed *(Genesis: 6)*. Yes, I truly believed that I was walking on very thin ice.

Somehow, my very intuitive, ninety year old mother-in-law must have noticed my struggle. She saw how lost, confused, and depressed I was, so she gave me a NIV Life Application Study Bible. I realize now that this was God's hand at work in my life because He knew I needed answers that I could only find there.

I began to read that Bible every day and I began to pray frequently. One of the first stories that I read was the story of the prodigal son. *(Luke 15: 11-32)* This story revealed to me a loving God that was waiting patiently for me to return to Him and confess my sins. I did so with a humble heart. I asked God to forgive me for being so stupid and sinful...for thinking that I knew better than He...for thinking that I could control my life and my destiny...for thinking that I didn't need Him. I asked Him to forgive me for being angry with Him because He didn't answer prayers the way I thought He should answer them. I simply asked Him to lead me where He wanted me to be. I surrendered myself to Him and His will for my life.

According to the scripture in *(Luke 15: 11-32)* He rejoiced in my return and made me an heir to His kingdom! He was waiting all those years to welcome me home and wipe away my sins. I felt that I was making 'baby steps' in the right direction at this point. *"Ask and it will be given to you; knock and the door will be opened to you; seek and you shall find." (Matthew 7:7)* I knew I had a long way to go to find my way back to God, but at least I had started my journey.

Chapter Nine

Family Tragedy

When we are grieving the loss of a loved one, I think it is normal to revisit conversations and events in our mind that somehow help us to process that grief. That was certainly true in my case. I started remembering conversations that Jimmy and I had over the past few years since the loss of our Mother and after his divorce when he moved to Florida. In retrospect, I now realize that Jimmy knew his time here was running out.

"Do you ever think about death?" He asked one day out of the clear blue.

"I guess I have…no more than anyone else," I answered.

"Do you ever wonder what really happens to us when we take that last breath," he continued.

"I've just always assumed that whatever happens to one… happens to all of us," I volunteered.

"When Mom died, I think I started to really wonder for the first time in my life," he continued. "I've lost a lot of friends over the years, our sister, and even our Dad, but none of their deaths caused me to think like hers did."

"I know," was all I could manage to reply.

"Do you remember when you and I kept a constant vigil by her bedside when she was dying?" he asked.

"Yes, of course I do."

"I remember how the doctors and nurses always commented on how much she looked like an angel lying there when they walked into her room and she was sleeping," he went on. "She did look angelic, or spiritual, or something that I can't describe. There was almost a glow around her that everyone could see. She looked like she was filled with Jesus Himself. Do you remember that?"

"Yes, I do," I replied.

"I know if there is a heaven, she is definitely there," he continued.

"The part that amazed me was that she was never in any pain and she never had any pain meds...I have to agree with you on that one. If there is a God and heaven, she is right there with Him," I finished.

"I know Faye is there in heaven with her," he said. When she died, I think I lost all faith in God. Then when they came out with drugs that could have controlled her seizures less than a year after her death," he continued, "I was so angry with God. She was such a good girl...never missed a Sunday in church...she sang in the choir...she taught Sunday school Class...she had a heart of gold and always lived her life to glorify God."

Our sister, Faye, who was only two years older than Jimmy was diagnosed with epilepsy at the age of thirteen. Unfortunately, there were no medications at that time that would control her seizures, so the entire family always kept a vigilant watch over her to make sure that she didn't get hurt when these seizures occurred and to make sure that she didn't asphyxiate. She was twenty-one years old and married with a two year old daughter when she asphyxiated in her sleep with her little girl snuggled up to her.

"I know," was all I could manage to say. I knew what a loss my entire family had suffered when she died, but it really took a toll on Jimmy. Together, the two of them had helped our mother with the younger children in our family including me, and they shared a bond that the rest of us could never join.

I drifted into my own thoughts as I remembered that early morning phone call like it was yesterday. My Mother answered the phone and we could see from the expression on her face that something was horribly wrong. The person on the other end had just informed her that Faye had been found dead in her bed. My Mother was in such denial that she insisted that we all go on to school because she was certain that by the time we returned home from school this mistake would be completely cleared up and we would find that our sister was perfectly fine. I remember walking to school praying to God that my Mother was right and that I would return home to find that my sister was safe and alive. This would be one of many prayers that were never answered. At the tender age of eight, I felt myself becoming angry with God, so I certainly could relate to the feelings that Jimmy was sharing with me.

After this unfathomable tragedy, our Mother chose to cling to God knowing that somehow this was all part of His plan. She was comforted by the thought that Faye was now at peace with God and she would never be plagued with those horrible seizures again. She also firmly believed that she would see her daughter again when she herself passed from this life. My Father chose a predictable route for himself. He decided that the only answers or comfort he needed could be found in the bottom of the next bottle of liquor that he consumed.

"I think that is when I decided that God didn't really exist." Jimmy said as he broke into my own personal thoughts. "How could He? He showed no mercy or love when He left her little two year old daughter motherless," he added teary eyed.

"I think her death affected me more than I realized until much later," I said reflectively. "I never dreamed I would live past the age of twenty-one for some reason. Even though I didn't have anything wrong with me, I just felt that I would not survive....then I realized only the good die young, so that took care of that problem," I laughed. "I don't know why I gave up on God...I guess I prayed too many prayers that were never answered or at least not answered the way I wanted."

"I'm sure Mom prayed a lot of prayers over both of us...we both got so far off the spiritual track that she raised us on...we must have really disappointed her," he added.

"I don't think we disappointed her at all! She loved us very much!" I argued.

Even though Jimmy was my big brother and my hero, I soon learned that he had a very dark, secret side that he very carefully and slowly revealed to me.

Chapter Ten

Past Demons Revealed

Jimmy always loved it when I took a break from traveling in the motor home and decided to spend time at the condo. I remember a particular break from the motor home in 2007 when my son picked me up at the airport and dropped me off at my condo. He was surprised to find that Jimmy had already been there to check on everything. He had turned my air conditioner down to 72 degrees so it would be nice and cool when I arrived, opened all the blinds, and just made sure that everything was as it should be. He had even stocked my refrigerator with my favorite wine, milk, and sodas. No one could ask for a better brother or friend.

I saw the message light blinking on the phone and I knew it was another message from Jimmy. "Hey, this is your 'big brother.' Call me when you get in. Love Ya!" Every message he ever left me started off with '*Hey, this is your big brother!*'

I picked up the phone and called Jimmy's house. The phone rang and rang then the voice mail picked up. I left a message saying that I was at the condo, but I was going to try his cell phone. I called his cell phone and it went straight to voice mail. Not thinking much about it, I decided to jump in the shower and get ready for our usual dinner together. I felt sure we would go out, since I had nothing on hand to cook.

I showered, got dressed, and tried his phones again; still no answer on either one. That seemed odd to me because he always had his cell phone with him and it was always on and charged. I decided that I would just drive over to his house to make sure that everything was ok.

By this time, it was early evening and the sun was just starting to set. The sky was a beautiful pink as the sun, like a giant fire ball, went down into the waters of the Gulf of Mexico. Sea gulls were flying all around making their calling noise. Even the brown pelicans were soaring overhead as if to welcome me home. The sea breeze was warm and gentle against my face as I opened my car door and jumped in. I was struck by the incredible beauty of the place that I called home.

I hurried over to Jimmy's house not daring to let myself think that something could possibly be wrong. The evening was just simply too gorgeous for anything to be wrong anywhere I thought to myself as I pulled into his driveway. His truck was there, but there were no lights on inside. I walked to the front door and turned the handle. It was locked. I rang the doorbell and waited to see if I could hear any activity inside…nothing. I had a key to his house on my key ring, so I let myself in. As I walked inside I turned on the light in the foyer and called his name. No answer. I kept walking through the house turning on lights and calling his name. When I got to the family room, I saw him sitting in his recliner slumped over and I almost screamed. I didn't know if he was dead or alive, but I checked for a heartbeat and found one. He started to stir a little as I was checking to see if I could find any obvious problem with him. "Hey, Sis... When did you get here?" he mumbled.

"Jimmy, how long have you been in this chair like this," I asked him ignoring his question.

"Don't know," was all he could say.

"I'm going to call an ambulance," I said more to myself than to him.

"No, I'm ok....I don't need to go to the hospital," he almost whispered.

"Yes, I think you do," I snapped.

"No, not an ambulance....you can drive me to the emergency room."

"Jimmy, I don't think I can get you into the car...can you get up?"

"Yes... just give me a minute."

I don't know how we managed to do it, but we got him into my vehicle and to the emergency room. Once we were there, I stopped the car in front of the emergency room door and ran inside. I practically screamed that someone had to help me get my brother out of the car. Immediately, a young man in a white coat pulled a wheel chair out of nowhere and followed me to the waiting car outside.

All I could think about was what would have happened to him if I had not just happened to be in town that day. As it turned out, he was in renal failure. He had a long history of kidney problems stemming back several years when a doctor in Georgia had removed an embedded kidney stone and punctured his kidney. His kidneys had been very weak since that time. This particular time a kidney stone was blocking the urethra so his body was shutting down

After several days in the hospital, I could tell that Jimmy was feeling much better because he was telling jokes and flirting with all the nurses and conversing with anyone that he could engage in conversation. I spent most of every day there with him, but I could never get in there early enough to have a conversation with his doctor. I only got second hand reports from Jimmy, and according to what he told me, the doctor seemed to think all was normal and he could resume his usual schedule as soon as he was released.

When they finally released him from the hospital, I tried to get him to come home with me for a few days, but he insisted that he go to his home. I finally gave in and decided that I would spend as much time there with him as possible. Surely, he would be all right at night when I went home to sleep. Jimmy and I always enjoyed spending hours together talking about everything from politics and current events to family issues and just about anything else that could be imagined.

This particular day our conversation started out almost as gloomy as the rainy, overcast day outside. He quietly started this conversation reflectively, "I look back over my life and I see what a mess I made of it. I was messed up practically from the beginning…I remember when I was about ten or eleven years old and Dad would take me with him to see one of his girlfriends… I saw and heard things that I shouldn't have…he would just make me promise not to tell Mom!" he sighed. "I always felt so guilty every time I looked into Mom's eyes because of the secrets that I had to keep from her."

Our mother was the daughter of a teacher and the Granddaughter of a Baptist Minister. When she was two years old, her father died as a result of the Flu epidemic of 1920. Her mother, who was half Cherokee Indian, took her two little girls and ran away from her husband's family because they insisted that she marry one of the single brothers to make sure that the children were properly cared for and educated as was the custom in the south at that time.

Our Father was the illegitimate son of a rich, handsome tobacco heir. His Father had a family complete with a wife and several children that lived and thrived in South Carolina never suspecting that my Father and his sister existed. His mother, who we were never allowed to call Grandmother, had been born and raised on a plantation in Georgia called Pine Knot which probably explains why she had that 'Scarlett O'Hara complex that I remember so well as a child. She was also from a well-to-do family, so I can only imagine the scandal that must have occurred in their area when my father and his sister were born. That may also explain why she insisted on being called 'Miss Jewel' instead of Grandmother.

How our parents ever decided to get married and have a family has always been a mystery to me. I finally decided that my mother probably thought she could save my father's soul and maybe he thought he could give her the family she had lost. Whatever the reason, it turned out to be a prescription for a totally dysfunctional family on almost every level.

"Good grief, Jimmy," was all I could respond as I came back to our conversation.

"Then," he continued, "I was about twelve years old when my teacher molested me at school the first time."

"You have to be kidding me," I exclaimed. "What happened?"

"When the other kids went outside for recess, she would take me into the coat closet and do things to me…she would make me do things to her… It started out innocently enough. At first, she would just kiss me and I would kiss her back…then she started making me rub her breast...then she took off her blouse and bra...gradually she was completely undressed and so was I. Well, you know where it eventually ended?"

"Did you tell our parents?" I asked.

"No, I just thought it was just another day at school. It went on the entire school year like that."

"Jimmy, that breaks my heart...That certainly explains why you have had such a problem with commitment and relationships," I offered. "Why didn't you say something to Mom?"

"Oh, that wasn't the only times...There was a gorgeous blonde woman in the neighborhood that became friendly with me. I cut her grass for her and she bought me comic books, but that eventually turned sexual as well," he said. "She was a gorgeous blonde with a body that any male would appreciate," he continued. "By that time I was quite experienced thanks to my teacher, so she didn't have to do very much to get my attention! I soon learned when her husband would be working and when I could visit. Once, I knocked on her door and her husband answered! He just about scared me to death, but she quickly came to the door and rescued me. She was in a very thin nighty that left nothing to the imagination, but she just smiled and told me that I could cut the lawn tomorrow. I guess her husband bought that little act because he didn't say anything to me. I went back the next day and we just proceeded with our usual activity like nothing had ever happened! She did tell me that I should watch for a red vase sitting in the front window if her husband was home. She showed me exactly where she would place the vase each day when he was home, and she said she would remove it from the window as soon as he left every day. That way I wouldn't be confronted by him again. After that, I was always afraid that he would come home while we were in the bedroom, so that made for some pretty tense times with her. Fortunately, somehow Mom figured it out and paid her a visit. Mom told her that if she ever spoke to or looked at me again, she would inform the woman's husband. That took care of that situation."

"Jimmy, I am so sorry that you had to go through that…including the things that our Dad put you through. All of that was child abuse...you were the victim," I stated.

"I don't think of myself as a victim...I just figured it was part of being a male. As a matter of fact, Dad said to me once, *"don't miss one, you might miss a good one!"*

"That's just disgusting!" I yelled. "He was such a loser. I don't know how our mother stayed with him all those years...I guess I do know the answer to that. She told me that after he had the stroke that partially paralyzed him... she couldn't just put him out on the street. "

That day will forever be etched in my brain because it changed my family's future forever. My Dad had been complaining of a blinding headache for a couple of days and apparently nothing that he took for it helped. When we returned from church that Sunday, he had just gotten out of bed and was in the kitchen getting ready to make pancakes. He asked if we all wanted some, and of course, we were thrilled that he was even in the kitchen doing this. I was in the kitchen with him happy to see that he was obviously feeling better. Then all of a sudden, he dropped the glass measuring cup to the floor, he grabbed the corner of the counter, and he started sinking to the floor. As he went down to the floor, he was calling for his mother, Miss Jewel, who was in the dining room next to the kitchen. By the time she got to him, he was completely unconscious on the floor. Eventually the ambulance arrived to take him to the hospital. As the ambulance pulled away, I remember standing there crying and praying that God would take care of him and somehow save him. I felt that God failed me and my family. That was a feeling that would repeat itself several times in my life.

My Dad didn't die, but he was left completely paralyzed on his right side and unable to speak from the effects of the stroke that he had. The day that he was brought home from the hospital was the day that I realized how drastically my family would be changed forever. There was no such thing as disability insurance or any of the other social safety nets that our society has in place now. My Father would never be able to work again or provide for our family in any way. He basically needed around the clock care for a very long time. I can't speak for my siblings, but at this point in my life, I was completely over God. He had yet again deserted me and my family. I was only twelve years old.

It was at this time in my life that my newly found hero, my big brother, stepped up and made all the difference in my life as well as the other three children left at home.

"I know," he sighed.

"I guess I see how all that could have affected my early years when I was stationed in Germany and when I started working at General Motors. Man, talk about partying. I went to bed with anything that moved," he laughed. I remember hanging out with John Delorean, who was an engineer at GM at that time; GM flew us all over the country and we just did anything we wanted to do…all on the company dime! Toni would have divorced me years ago if she had only known all the stuff I did back then."

Jimmy had started to work at General Motors on the assembly line shortly after returning from the army in the mid 50's. He went to college at night and gradually worked his way up to an executive position in a few short years. He said that he was born into a poor family, but he had no intentions of living his life like that.

"I remember that you were friends with Delorean before he left GM and started his own car company. I'm sure he was quite the scoundrel," I smiled.

"Yeah, as a matter of fact, after I lost my court case against GM in the early 90's, I was contacted by a publishing company to tell all that I knew about General Motors…about the corruption…the hot shots…"

Even though Jimmy had made a full recovery after a minor stroke in the mid 90's, GM forced him into early retirement. He filed an age discrimination suit against GM that he should have won, but his lawyer was negligent causing Jimmy to have a very real distrust of lawyers after that.

"Why didn't you do that?"

"I almost did. We had negotiated all the terms of the contract…They were going to put me up in a mountain cabin in the middle of the woods somewhere, give me a ghost writer, and pay all the expenses. I almost did it, but then I thought about all the things I would have to reveal about myself to tell that story…I don't think my kids should know all of that stuff."

"Jimmy, your kids are grown. I'm sure they have done some pretty ridiculous things themselves. Besides, what could you possibly have done that could be so horrible?" I asked. "You've never killed anyone, have you?"

"Well…I'm not sure how to answer that," he went on. "I have paid for so many abortions I lost count…. I even performed a couple of them myself…"

"You have to be kidding me! How do you know how to perform an abortion?"

"Well, this was back in the 50's before abortion was legalized, so we just had to do what we had to do…"

"My gosh, you didn't kill any of those girls, did you?"

"No," he laughed. "They all survived, but abortions were performed in dirty back rooms, under some pretty bad circumstances…"

"You watched the procedures?" I asked.

"How do you think I learned how to do it?"

"I can't believe I'm asking this, but what did you do? I asked.

"You just take a coat hanger and…"

"No, stop! I don't want to hear this," I gasped.

"I've told you before that your big brother was not a very good guy!"

"You are a good guy. You're just the product of a dysfunctional background," I said trying to make him feel better about this burden he had been carrying around for decades. "Did Mom know about any of this?"

"No, after I got Connie pregnant and Phyllis was born, I just decided that I couldn't have any more kids. I couldn't afford them… and help take care of my brothers and sisters."

Connie was Jimmy's first wife that he married basically because he got her pregnant right after he returned from the army. My mother insisted that he marry her and try to make a bad situation right. As it turned out, the marriage was over before she actually gave birth to his daughter, Phyllis. Apparently, it was an experience that shaped a lot of future decisions that he made.

"Did you ever think about abstinence or using a condom?" I almost whispered to him. He just looked at me and smiled knowing that I had struck a nerve. "That makes me wonder how many illegitimate kids our Dad fathered…or how many abortions he paid for…That's exactly why I had to marry someone from a different state. I wanted to make sure I wasn't tapping into the same gene pool!" I said laughingly.

"I think that was a wise decision on your part, Sis." He sighed instead of laughing as I had expected.

"I think you and Dad both were just too good looking for your own good and obviously, not very respectful of women in general." I said.

Later that evening as I sat alone, I couldn't help but think about the awful confessions Jimmy had made. Our Dad was a scoundrel and we all knew it, but I was still stunned to think how much Jimmy turned out like him. That was the one thing that he never wanted to do. At least Jimmy didn't seem to have Dad's abusive nature. Little did I know that this was just the tip of the ice berg of things that he would confess to me. I made up my mind right then and there that I was not going to be judgmental about anything that he had told me that night or any other confessions that he felt compelled to make. He could not do anything to make me stop loving him or seeing the good in him. I knew him better than he knew himself and I loved him unconditionally.

Jimmy's first school picture estimated age is 5 to 6 yrs. old

Jimmy's last Shriner Picture taken approximately 2006

Jimmy with me when I was only one in 1949 in front of the home that my mother and father built with their own hands

From left to right John, Lee, Jayne, and Jimmy

Jimmy's Harley that he rode in the Shriner's parades

Jimmy proudly served his country as a Paratrooper in the 50's

Chapter Eleven

God's Mercy

Shortly after Christmas, February 27th to be exact, was Jimmy's birthday. The pain on that day was overwhelmingly sad. This would be the first birthday of his that I would have to celebrate alone. In the past, we had always celebrated our birthdays together if I happened to be in town at that time, but not this time or...ever again. The stark reality of my loss was so great that words can't even describe how I felt that day. I realized then that birthdays would never be a joyous time for me again.

Sheldon Vanauken wrote in *A Severe Mercy*, "*It is not the grief, involving that momentary reality, that cuts one off from the beloved but the void that is loss. In the end one can no longer summon forth that reality, and then one's tears dry up. But while it lasts, it is a shield against the void; and by the time the grief wanes, the terrible emptiness of loss has given way to a new world that does not contain the shape of the beloved figure.*" How I longed for that 'new world.'

Right about that time, I had a routine dermatologist visit for rosacea which I had been dealing with for years. While I was sitting in the reception room waiting for my name to be called, I glanced through the literature there on skin cancer. I already knew that I was a high risk because I was very fair skinned, had lots of moles, had spent a lifetime in the sun without protection, and had even been known to get a quick tan by going to the tanning salons. I realized as I sat there reading that information that I probably should ask the doctor about it and make that much dreaded appointment to be completely checked out.

When she completed the rosacea exam, I nonchalantly asked her about scheduling a full body scan for skin cancer. She said, "I have time now, if you do?"

That caught me a little off guard, but I followed her instructions, stripped down, and put on the paper dressing gown as I nervously waited for her to return and start the examination. She was very thorough and quite frankly a little scary. She circled several sites on my back, legs, and arms. She tried to assure me that she just felt we should do routine biopsies just to be on the safe side. When she was all finished, I had a total of seventeen biopsies done! As I left the office, I was assured that they would have the results in a few days and not to worry. I fought the urge to rush home and Google skin cancer and read all the information that I could find.

Two days later, my phone rang and 'caller ID' identified it was the dermatology office. I almost choked as I answered the phone. "Hello," I managed to squeak.

"Hi, this is Susan at the dermatology office," she explained in a superficially happy voice. "The doctor would like for you to come in tomorrow to discuss your biopsies, if that is convenient for you?"

"Uh, I guess so...yes, I can make that. Were they alright?" I asked almost afraid of the answer.

"I'm sorry, I don't have that information. She just asked that I make the call and get you in right away."

"Wow, that is scary," I added. "Can we make it first thing in the morning? I don't want to sit around worrying about this all day."

"Of course we can. How does 8:00 a.m. sound to you?"

"I will be there," I choked. "Thank you."

I don't think I slept at all that night because I was pouring my heart out to God. Was this going to be His wrath that I feared so much? I read and reread *"When I am afraid, I will put my trust in You."* (Psalm 56:3) Consequently, getting there for that appointment was not a problem. I actually arrived before they unlocked the door to let patients in! They took me right in for my consultation with her. She tried very hard not to frighten me, but that train had already left the station.

After our cordial greetings she began, "Jayne, three of the biopsies came back as Melanoma. Three others were what we call pre-Melanoma. Fortunately, the Melanoma is only a stage one, so they can be removed and no further action will need to be taken." As I sat there in a complete state of shock she continued, "I am going to suggest that you be rechecked every three months to make sure there is no recurrence. I also want to make sure that you get your blood work done at least once a year and a chest X-ray. You already see your gynecologist annually and have a mammogram done, don't you?"

"Yes, I do."

"It is going to be very important that you keep doing that. You are very blessed that you made the decision to get checked out when you did," she added. "It is always easier to take care of something like this when it is very small rather than wait until it has spread to other parts of your body."

"I didn't make the decision. I think it was God's decision," I said fighting back tears and remembering that tiny little voice inside me that encouraged me to discuss it with the doctor. "So, when do we do this?"

"You can come back this afternoon, or we can wait a few days if you like," she said as she put her arm around my shoulder. "Fortunately, this will be an office procedure, so you will only have a local anesthetic. It won't be complicated at all."

"No, I think I want this out of me right now. I will come back this afternoon. Do I need to have someone drive me or will I be able to do this by myself?" I asked.

"If you have someone that can drive you, that might be better for you," she smiled. "Do you have any questions?" she asked.

"No, I think I'm just ready to get this over," I replied.

As I left her office that morning, tears were flooding down my cheeks. All I could think was, *'Thank you, God. Are you really taking care of me and watching over me even though I don't deserve it? Did You actually spare me Your wrath?'*

With God's help, I made it through the Melanoma scare and found that my faith was growing more each day. I noticed a difference in Mike as well.

We didn't discuss it very much, but I could tell that he was beginning to trust God more. We still had a long way to go to get back to Him, but we were making 'baby steps' on that journey back to God.

Things got a lot worse, but somehow I managed to nurture my new found faith. My prayer always seemed to end with the plea for God to lead us to exactly where He wanted us to be. I had no idea what that was going to look like, but I made the decision that I was going to trust God.

Mike managed to find a sales job about an hour away from our condo. Unfortunately, it was straight commission pay and nobody in Florida seemed to be buying anything at that time. We gradually depleted most of our cash reserves, sold everything that we could get rid of, cashed in his retirement, and cut our living expenses to the bare minimum, but we still couldn't stay ahead of the wolf at the door.

I continued to read my Bible daily and pray. I was still struggling with the loss of my 'big brother,' depression, and confusion, but Mike was the only person that knew about Jimmy's visit and how I was trying to cope with it all. I would read and reread the notes that I jotted down that morning after his visit trying to make some sense out of it and trying to figure out what it all meant. Somewhere deep inside of me, I kept hearing a little voice that told me this message was not just for me. Little did I know that before long this little voice would grow louder and louder.

Along the way, I was able to develop some coping skills that helped me deal with the sadness that seemed to swallow me up at times. I figured out that I could replace sad thoughts of Jimmy with a memory that was of happier times. I found comfort in wearing his Army ring around my neck on a chain, and I would spend hours looking at his collectable light houses that were given to me by his children after his death. Hours were spent in solitude looking at old photographs that were taken at various times in his life. I sometimes wondered if I would ever get past this feeling of loss.

Chapter Twelve

Big Brother Knows Best

I had so many memories of times that Jimmy and I shared, and many memories of times that he protected me from things that neither one of us could have possibly predicted. One such memory occurred several years ago when I was getting ready to go to the airport to rejoin Mike and the motor home. Jimmy came in and laid an envelope on my kitchen counter. "Do you and Mike have road side service for the motor home?" he asked.

"No…why?"

"You really ought to sign up for it because it is very expensive if you have an emergency and you're not covered," he stated.

"Mike keeps the motor home in really good condition…"

"That doesn't matter. You could have a blowout, or a mechanical problem that is totally unforeseen," he continued. "It costs a fortune to have someone tow a motor home in for repairs, or to come out and check the problem for you," he went on.

"I don't think we need it," I insisted.

"Okay, now it's my turn to be the pain in the rear," he laughed. It's not that expensive and I insist that you do it. Here is the paper work right here," he said as he handed me the envelope from the counter. "All you have to do is call the 800 number and they will sign you up over the phone. You'll be covered before you leave here."

"I'll look at it later," I said.

"No, I'm going to stand right here and watch you do this…if I don't, you'll just throw it in the trash and never give it another thought," he grumbled.

I took the envelope from his hand and looked over the information. It wasn't that expensive, so I picked up the phone and started the application process. Before I hung up with the person on the other end, they gave me a member number to keep with me until our permanent cards came in the mail. Thanking the customer service representative, I hung up the phone and said to Jimmy, "Are you satisfied?"

"Now I am," he laughed. That one little act would prove to be a reminder to me of just how much my big brother always had my back and always looked out for me.

Jimmy drove me to the airport where I flew to Houston to meet Mike and start our journey back to California. He had to be at the annual industry trade show before it began the following weekend in Southern California. A lot of preparation goes into setting up one of those shows, and he always liked to be involved from the ground up. He had already picked the equipment that would be used for the display and the transportation for all of it had already been arranged. Now, it would just be setting everything up at the show site and making sure that all the sales people were apprised of their roles and responsibilities. This was always stressful for Mike, but fun and rewarding at the same time.

We decided that we would leave early Monday morning and allow ourselves plenty of time to get there so Mike didn't have to drive that huge motor home for more than eight to ten hours each day. Of course, we didn't get out of Houston as early as we wanted, but that always seemed to be the case. We had made that trip west across Texas so many times before that we knew every place to stop for diesel, and any staple supplies we needed. We even knew the exits to avoid because the motor home was too large to get in and out easily. Safety was always a priority for us when we stopped somewhere overnight.

On that first day of driving, we didn't get as far across Texas as we had wanted, but it was not a problem because we allowed ourselves extra time. The second day, Mike received a call that there was a problem with the space we had leased for the show, so he realized that he needed to get there quicker than we had anticipated. Consequently, he decided to drive as late as he could that second night. Everything was going smoothly as we drove through the Arizona desert that night.

Midnight on that stretch of highway is very dark and lonely. Occasionally, we were passed by a semi-truck, or met one coming in the opposite direction. The temperature in the desert was very warm that night, but we remained very comfortable because of the motor home's very efficient air conditioner. Mike and I just continued on into the night as we had done so many times before never suspecting that this time was going to be considerably different.

All of a sudden while driving 70 miles per hour, the lights inside and outside of the motor home went dark. The engine stopped, and I could tell that Mike had lost the power steering because he was struggling to coast the huge vehicle off the road and onto a narrow shoulder. The strain and fear of being in total darkness, and I do mean total darkness, was extremely unnerving for me. Furthermore, I could not imagine being behind the wheel of this huge vehicle when it just died. Not only was it really dark, but nothing on the motor home was working; nothing but the air brakes! Somehow, the speed we had been traveling helped Mike coast the vehicle off the road. Once we were safely on the side of the road, I was frightened to see how totally black it was outside; there was no moon, no stars...Not a light in sight except for the occasional semi that flew past us rocking and shaking the motor home like it was a toy. Those semis were so close we could have reached out and touched them. More frightening yet was the fact that they could not see us because we had no lights at all.

The first thing Mike did was go outside with our 'earthquake radio' that had a flashing light on it. He walked about fifty yards behind the motorhome to place some type of light there to prevent those semis from hitting us, but the grass was over a foot high. He mashed the grass down so the flashing light could be visible to the on-coming traffic. As he walked back to the door of the motor home, I shined the light I was holding to help him see as he slowly navigated his way back to the door. There was no way I was going out there to meet him. He said the whole time he was out there all he could think about was this is Arizona…rattle snake country!

He made it back inside, took the emergency flash light that we kept in the front of the motor home and stepped back into the dry hot desert night to look around and see if he could figure out what our problem was. As he approached the back of the motor home to check the huge batteries that are located there, a couple of trucks flew past us much too close for comfort, and I couldn't help but notice that we were just barely off the paved road. The shoulder had a big drop off, so we could not have pulled over any farther even if the motor home could have coasted longer. The mirrors on the motor home protrude extensively, so they were only inches from the road. I was really concerned that one of those trucks might pass too close and knock the one on the driver's side off. I voiced that concern to Mike when he returned to the inside. He informed me that was the least of our worries. "I'm afraid that they won't be able to see us at all and run into the motor home," he said as he closed the door behind him. He didn't need to say anything else. I had a vivid image in my mind of those big rigs swerving and running off the road. That was all I could think about.

"Our batteries are completely dead," he announced sounding more than a little stressed.

"Great," was all I could manage to say. Then, I remembered that I had just paid for the road side service that Jimmy had insisted that I purchase before I left Florida. "Mike, we have road side service!" I exclaimed. As I fumbled around in the dark looking for the policy number and the phone number to call, I explained to him how Jimmy had practically twisted my arm and forced me to call the insurance company to pay for this service.

"I just hope we have phone service here," he said as he took the information from my hand. He found his phone, and I could tell that he was holding his breath as he checked to see if he had a signal. I saw him punching in the numbers on the phone, so I knew everything was going to be okay. I let out a sigh of relief as I made a mental note to thank Jimmy for his insistence. This could have been a nightmare for sure.

I sat quietly while Mike explained to the person on the other end of the phone that we were sitting in the desert miles from any service centers, and he was pretty sure that it was our batteries that caused the whole problem. After discussing the problem for about twenty minutes and getting the size and number off the batteries, the operator told him that because of where we were located it would be at least two to three hours before someone could get to us with any assistance. With the batteries bad, we could not start the generator, so we still had no power and no air conditioning. It was really hot! We opened up all the windows and shades hoping that would help cool things off, but the only breeze we had was from the scary big rigs as they went past at 70-75 miles per hour! We decided that we would try to get some sleep as we waited for help to arrive and hope that a truck didn't slam into us from the rear end! There was no way I could sleep with that threat looming.

After about 45 minutes, a highway patrol car pulled up behind us with his flashing lights on. He saw our little flashing light Mike had put out there and thought he had better check on us. Mike met him at the door and joined him outside. He explained that we had emergency road service coming, but our emergency flares had expired and did not work; all we had was that little emergency flashing light. The patrolman said he could help with that and put flares out behind us so we could be visible to the on-coming traffic. He said the flares he had would not last all night, but they should be good enough until help arrived. With that problem solved, maybe now we could actually get some sleep while waiting for help to arrive.

Still there was only the breeze from the passing trucks, but Mike stretched out in his recliner taking advantage of this opportunity to take a quick nap, and I decided to try to sleep on the couch. It was still unnerving every time a semi flew past because it would shake the motor home fiercely and their lights would illuminate the inside. Because it was so hot, we could not close the shades, so we would just have to ignore the lights. It was difficult for me to fall asleep, but Mike was asleep before he closed his eyes.

I found myself just lying there watching the shadows that were cast as each truck flew past us. I was almost asleep when another truck came flying past and I noticed the shadow on the ceiling over Mike's head. Earlier I had noticed that the light fixture over the kitchen table cast a shadow on the ceiling and that was no surprise. This shadow was! There was no light fixture over Mike's recliner, so what could possibly be causing that huge shadow? I didn't want to turn on my flash light because I didn't want to disturb Mike, so I patiently sat there and waited for another truck to pass by. Finally one came, and I was able to see that the shadow was moving, and it was a huge spider that appeared to me to be six to eight inches in diameter poised directly over Mike's head as he slept with his mouth wide open!

Now, that might not be a problem for most people, but I suffer from a lifelong condition called arachnophobia. That's just a fancy term for someone that is scared to death of spiders. Especially huge ones! My first instinct was to let out a blood curdling scream, but I knew that would probably cause Mike to have a heart attack (which would not be a viable option), so I gently reached over, touched Mike, and woke him up. I managed to tell him that there was a huge spider over his head on the ceiling. I must have fainted after that because I have no recollection of how Mike handled that spider. He said he looked up and immediately closed his mouth!

Our uninvited guest turned out to be a tarantula that must have hitched a ride into the motor home on Mike as he went in and out the door. Mike just used a paper towel and threw him outside in the grass. Both the tarantula and I survived our ordeal!

The next thing that I remember was someone knocking on the motor home door to assist us with our mechanical problem. It was in fact the batteries that caused the problem, but only one of them needed to be replaced. The technician switched out the battery, so we only had to pay for that because Jimmy had insisted on that road-side assistance policy which covered the two hour drive for the wrecker both ways and the labor cost. Then we were on our way again. Mike was amazed that we had road side service to cover that little incident, and I told him that he must make sure that he thanked Jimmy for that insight. That one mishap would have cost us more than three years' worth of premiums not to mention a lot of unnecessary hassle. Needless to say, Jimmy was delighted that he had insisted that I purchase that insurance, but the spider incident was hilarious to him! I really enjoyed hearing him laugh so hard he almost couldn't breathe.

Chapter Thirteen

Lean On Me

Jimmy always had a way of being there for me when I needed him most. For example, a few years ago, I was really suffering from allergies and breathing problems. A thorough examination by the allergist and an ear, nose, and throat specialist confirmed that I had polyps in one side of my sinus cavity and a deviated septum on the other side. The doctor was amazed that I could breathe at all. Of course the deviated septum was something that I was born with, but had not had any major problems until the polyps appeared on the other side because of allergies.

Naturally, I was scheduled for surgery. Mike came home to be with me during that time, but Jimmy made sure he was there as well. Looking back, I would have never done it if I had known how painful it was going to be.

When I woke up from the surgery, both Mike and Jimmy were right there probably thinking that I looked like I had been hit by a truck or something. My face was swollen; my eyes were black, and I had this plastic apparatus stuck up my nostril to help support the reconstruction of my septum. Usually, I have a very high pain tolerance, but I was in so much pain all I could do was cry.

Unfortunately, I don't tolerate pain meds very well, so this was going to be a very long two weeks! Mike took care of me the first couple of days, but then he had to return to work which meant he had to hop on a plane and fly back to the west coast. Mike felt sure that I was in good hands because Jimmy was going to be right there with me. Actually, I was in good hands.

He stayed the first few nights at the condo with me just to make sure that I was alright during the night. He did all the shopping for me and the laundry. He even fixed what few homemade meals he knew how to prepare. The rest of the time he would make sandwiches or pick up some kind of fast food.

After a few days, the pain subsided somewhat, but the plastic apparatus was still uncomfortable. Of course, I still looked like something in a horror show, but Jimmy didn't seem to mind. I avoided mirrors all together feeling very glad that Mike didn't have to stay with me.

It was times like this that Jimmy and I would always entertain each other with stories of our travels. Since we both had traveled extensively in our motor homes all over the country, we never ran out of tales to share. I began this story with, "Do you remember when we were traveling in the Eastern part of the country a couple of years ago?" I asked.

"Yes, I do," He replied.

"First of all, you need to know that Mike or I either one had ever been to Long Island, so we had no way of knowing what the driving conditions were like there...we just assumed that it was like every other place we had traveled in the U.S. Boy did we learn differently...We made it all the way to the Lincoln Tunnel without any problems at all, but when we pulled up to the tunnel about 3:00 in the afternoon, we were stopped by police officers and informed that we could not drive through there because we had a propane gas tank on board. I guess 911 changed a lot of things around New York. They assisted us traffic wise so that we could turn around and they even suggested an alternate route for us to take. We looked that up on our lap top computer and implemented the GPS function so that we would not have any difficulty following their instructions. It was a little stressful, but we were soon back on track and not even concerned that this detour was going to make us about an hour and a half late for our destination. We were sailing along without a care in the world. I was watching our progress on the lap top GPS and Mike was just driving along listening to the music. Then all of a sudden, Mike just gasped. I looked over at him and he was white as a sheet!

He said, *'Did you see that bridge we just went under?'*

'No,' I answered. *'What was wrong with it?'* I calmly asked."

'Our motor home is 12 feet 4 inches tall, and that bridge clearance was 12 feet 3 inches tall!' He practically screamed.

'Wow!' was all I could manage to say.

'If we hadn't been in the center lane as we went under it at 60 miles per hour, we wouldn't have cleared that thing!' His voice betrayed his stress and anxiety over our near miss. He said he thought all bridges were required to be over 13'6" on all major highways.

"With a sigh of relief, we continued on thinking nothing else about it. Then, all of a sudden Mike stopped in the middle of the eight lane highway directly in front of the next bridge that we came to. He was white as a ghost when he told me to look at the clearance posted in the center of the bridge. It said 9 feet 5 inches! If he had not been watching each bridge before he drove under it, we would have been decapitated by this one!"

"Wow, what did you do?" Jimmy asked.

"Well, the first thing we did was just sit there panicked as the cars were passing us on both sides blowing their horns, the drivers giving us the 'one finger salute', and both of us about as stressed out as we have ever been. Finally, Mike got his wits about him and he dialed 911. The operator came on the line and Mike explained our situation in great detail including reminding her that it was five o'clock traffic time on a Friday afternoon. She politely asked if anyone was injured and of course he answered that we were fine, but we were severely blocking traffic and people were very upset with us. She calmly informed Mike in her thick New York accent that she would get someone out to us as soon as possible. Forty Five minutes later, we were still sitting there with New Yorkers giving us their official 'welcome to New York' attitude and traffic backed up as far as the eye could see. About that time, an ambulance pulled up to Mike's window and asked if anyone was hurt. Once again, he answered with a little New York attitude of his own *'no...not yet!'* and was trying to ask where the police were, but before he could get anything out of his mouth the ambulance closed their window and quickly drove away!"

"Needless to say, Mike was livid! He just threw his hands up in the air and said, *'somebody just shoot me!'* About that time, a county utility truck pulled up along the shoulder of the road with his lights blinking so that everyone would get out of his way. The man got out of his truck, put on his orange vest and walked back to our motor home. I opened the door and let him in so that no one would run over him. He smiled at us, but I'm sure he was laughing like crazy on the inside and he said, *'I'm an RVer too, so I know how you must feel. It's getting dark here and you're in an area called 'little Jamaica' and they shoot people here for absolutely no reason at all!'*

"Well, that was all I needed to hear! Don't forget Mike had just uttered those exact words, *'somebody just shoot me!'* We explained how we had called 911 quite a while back and how the ambulance had come by and done nothing to help us. He was not the least bit surprised, but he offered to call a couple of police officers that were friends of his to see if they could help us out. As luck would have it, his friends were on duty. Eventually, we noticed that the traffic was not going past us anymore. If fact, the traffic stopped completely on our side of the eight lane highway. Then a police car pulled up beside us on Mike's side of the motor home. He kind of laughed as Mike apologized for the mess that we had caused and then he put us right at ease by saying, *'Thank God you stopped before you went under that thing. We've had that happen before and it takes hours to get the traffic cleared out and months to repair the bridge! Not to mention that you two would probably be dead now!'*

"He went on to explain that his fellow police officer had stopped the traffic all the way back to the last entrance ramp that fed the traffic onto the highway, and he asked if Mike could do a U-turn in the four lanes there. Of course he could, so the police officer led us through the U-turn to point us in the opposite direction that the traffic should flow on this side of the highway and we followed him all the way back to the on-ramp where we drove up the wrong way with him leading us. We were almost hysterical as we laughed uncontrollably releasing tension, relief, and every other emotion you can think of! When we were safely off the ramp and pointed in the right direction, both police officers joined us in the motor home and gave us a quick explanation of where we could drive the motor home on Long Island. They even went so far as to show us on our GPS all the details that would keep us safe in the future while we were guests there. Basically, they informed us that we had to avoid anything that said *Parkway*. That was probably the scariest, funniest, most frustrating thing that has ever happened to us," I concluded. He loved that story because he had lived in that area for years and knew exactly the peril that we had lived through.

Jimmy took me to my doctor's appointments and didn't even seem to be embarrassed to be seen in public with me. The day the doctor removed that apparatus stuck in my nostril was a day worth celebrating. Even though my eyes were still somewhat black, he took me to my favorite restaurant for dinner. Of course, he had to point out to everyone that both my eyes were still black! He laughingly told one couple,

"You should see the other girl!" He knew exactly how to embarrass me as any good brother is capable of doing.

Chapter Fourteen

Hind Sight is 20/20

Looking back on past conversations and events, I felt like a fool and more than a little guilty for not seeing the signs and hints that he dropped to let me know just how serious his health was becoming. He made the decision to make one last trip to Ohio to give his son his motor home. That should have made me realize then that something was very wrong. That one act meant that he was not only going to give up traveling which he loved, but he was no longer going to help with the Shriner's Circus which had been a huge part of his life forever especially after his retirement.

In addition, that last trip almost killed him. He drove the motor home up in late fall planning on staying with his son through Christmas, but it didn't work out quite like he had planned. After the long drive in the motorhome to reach Jim's house, Jimmy arrived there very ill. He was so ill that his son had to take him to the hospital where they admitted him. My nephew was extremely stressed out when he called to let me know that his Dad was in the hospital there. It was a combination of exhaustion, kidney, and liver problems that caused this emergency. He was hospitalized for two weeks. Again, I should have realized that his health was more fragile than I thought.

As soon as Jimmy was released from the hospital, he decided that he would just rest a couple of days and then fly home to Florida foregoing his plans to be with his son through Christmas. His son was so concerned about the two flight changes that he would have to make to fly home that he offered to drive him home, but the doctor said a road trip was more than Jimmy could handle. As a matter of fact, he should have never driven the motor home there in the first place. I should have realized then that the fall of 2007 was a foreshadowing of things to come.

Needless to say, I flew back home early for the holidays to be there with him when he arrived back in Florida and to make sure that he was all right. After picking up my vehicle from the condo, I went straight over to Jimmy's house. It was about 8:00 p.m. when I rang the doorbell. He answered the door with his usual enthusiasm, "Hi, Sis," he laughed. "You didn't have to rush home...I'm fine!"

"I know you are, but I just wanted an excuse to come home anyway," I laughed. When I walked inside, I could see that his place was a mess. Even though he had learned to cook a few things after his divorce, his housekeeping skills still needed some work. "Come on, I'll take you to dinner." I said.

I could tell he was still a little weak from his ordeal, but he seemed fine otherwise. When I dropped him off after dinner, I said, "Jimmy, I'm going to come over in the morning and help you clean your house, ok?"

"You don't have to do that. You have a lot you need to be doing to get ready for Thanksgiving and Christmas yourself. I will get to it eventually." He laughed.

"I know I don't have to do it, but I want to. Besides, by the time you get to it, the health department may condemn the place! With both of us working, it won't take very long at all. I'll see you in the morning."

He gave me a big hug and said, "Love ya! See you tomorrow."

The next morning, I knocked on his door about 9:00 a.m. To my surprise, he was still in bed. He came to the door in his pajamas and robe. "Are you ok?" I asked.

"Yeah, I just had a bad night," he answered. "I don't know why I get so hot at night. I wake up soaking wet with sweat. I had to get up and change my clothes and the sheets last night."

"Have you told the doctor about that?" I asked.

"No, it's not a big deal. Anyway, I'll get dressed and we can get started."

"Maybe your air conditioner isn't working right," I speculated.

"No, it's fine. It's just me. Maybe the cancer has spread all over my body…"

"Jimmy, you know that isn't the case. The doctor said that you are fine," I argued. I realize now that I should have paid more attention to what he was trying to tell me.

I went into the kitchen and made coffee while he got dressed. I had already had breakfast, but I fixed bagels and cream cheese for him. Shortly, he joined me in the kitchen and sat down while I toasted his bagel and got his coffee. We talked about nothing in particular while he finished his breakfast, then we got down to serious cleaning. I started in the kitchen cleaning out the refrigerator and freezer discarding what I call 'science projects.'

He got the vacuum cleaner out and started trying to vacuum. He spent most of his time working on and tinkering with the vacuum cleaner. He would push it a few times and then sit down and work on it some more. I eventually realized that this was his way of covering up the fact that he had no energy. Again, I should have paid closer attention.

I just kept cleaning and cleaning. I cleaned both bathrooms, completely sanitized the kitchen, swept and mopped the tile, dusted, did a few loads of laundry, and discarded a mountain of junk mail. Hours later, he still hadn't finished vacuuming the carpet, so I finished that task as well. When we were all finished, I told him I was going to call someone to cut the grass for him. He knew I couldn't do the lawn because of my allergy to grass. He, of course, didn't want me to, but I explained that he did not need to be outside trying to maintain a yard that was already out of control especially as weak as he was and the city would send him a bill for the fine that they would impose if the yard wasn't cared for properly. So, I won. When we were all finished, I asked if he wanted a glass of ice water. We sat in his family room sipping our well-deserved ice water and just relaxing. He was staring at two pictures of our mother that had been taken when she was in the hospital just before she died. "I still miss her," he said.

"Me too... Sometimes I can't believe that she is really gone. Can you believe it has been ten years already?" I choked

Then out of nowhere he said, "I thought about suicide."

"What?...When?" I asked.

"Remember when I had the stroke?" he asked.

"Yes..." I was so surprised by this revelation that I couldn't find words to continue.

"Right after the stroke, I was so depressed...then when GM forced me to retire, I became even more depressed," he continued. "I just remembered Dad and how he was left after his stroke. I couldn't bear living my life like that. Of course, I wasn't left paralyzed and speechless like he was, but I just felt useless...unproductive. Even though my children were grown and on their own, I didn't feel like I could be there for them if they needed me."

All I could do was sit and stare at him as he went on.

"I was just going to walk down by the lake behind the house and blow my brains out." He almost whispered.

"Why?" I finally asked.

"I just felt like I was losing myself...I was no longer me...I no longer had a purpose in life."

"I don't ever remember you being that depressed or suicidal at that time," I said.

"I did a good job of hiding it, didn't I?" he asked.

"I guess you did," I said in disbelief.

"So how did you get past that?" I questioned.

"I started seeing a psychiatrist that helped me a lot, I guess."

"He must have...you're still here," I joked. "Did Toni know that you were going through that...that you were having thoughts of suicide?" I asked.

"No, not at the time. I think she knew later," he answered.

After a long pause, he said, "I had that dream again."

"What dream?" I asked.

"You know the one where I saw my obituary and it said that I died at age 72."

"Jimmy, it's just a dream! You will be 72 in February and you are doing fine. The doctor said you are cancer free, your heart is good, and you even have your liver problems under control. You're only problem is that you just overdo it sometimes," I reminded him. "You need to remember that you are in your 70's now, and you can't do all the things you did when you were young. Please don't talk yourself into dying just because of some silly dream."

I wish now that I had believed him. I don't know how he knew, but he did. I have wondered if the doctor had given him a time frame, or if he had figured it out for himself, or maybe it had been some kind of precognition. I guess I will never know the answer to that, but I do know that I will carry that guilt in my heart forever because I didn't pay attention to what he was obviously trying to tell me.

Chapter Fifteen

First Anniversary of His Death

On the first anniversary of his death, November 8, 2009, I spent most of that day in prayer, and yes, a lot more tears were shed that day. I guess I did that because there were times in my grief that I was extremely concerned about Jimmy's soul. I knew that Jimmy was burdened with a lot of sin before he died and the more I read my Bible the more concerned I became. I'm almost positive that Jimmy was not in a good place spiritually when he died. To my knowledge, he never asked for God's forgiveness before he breathed his last breath. I wish I had known then what I know now. I would have prayed with him a prayer asking for God's forgiveness encouraging him to accept Jesus Christ as his Lord and Savior. My failure to do that will always be a huge burden on my heart because I feel like I let him down when he needed me the most. I can only hope that while he was comatose in the last days of his life perhaps God spoke to his heart and Jimmy was able to communicate with Him in a very private way unburdening his soul.

On this first anniversary of his death, I remembered something that he told me one night when he and I were having dinner at my condo that still weighs heavily on my heart. We began to talk about things that neither one of us had ever openly discussed before like our shared experiences growing up in a dysfunctional household, how we had suffered from the abusive father that we shared, and how it affected us when he would abuse our Mother or one of our siblings. We talked about the things that had motivated us to do some of the things we had done and the choices that we had made in life. Yes, we even discussed regrets that we had. It was probably one of the most honest and heart felt times I ever shared with my brother. I have never had someone bare their heart and soul to me as he did that night.

It started off light and jovial with me reminding him of the time in the late 50's when all the kids in the neighborhood came running up to me and screaming, "Elvis Presley is in your back yard!" Needless to say, we all took off running for my back yard, never thinking about the fact that Elvis would never, ever be near my back yard! We just knew that he was the most famous singer in the world and we wanted to see him! As we ran up the driveway to my back yard, I saw Jimmy doing something to his Chevrolet convertible parked there!

"There he is!" screamed one of my little friends.

"You dummy!" I yelled. "That's just my brother, Jimmy!" I must admit, he did look a lot like Elvis, and of course, he never tired of hearing that story. He and Elvis also shared one other thing. Jimmy loved peanut-butter-banana sandwiches just as much as the *King* if not more!

The conversation gradually moved to a more serious tone as he began by asking me if I remembered Marie, one of his old girl friends from his youth. Of course I remembered her because she and her daughter had visited Jimmy at his home just a couple of years ago. I just happened to be in town at the time, so I was able to meet her again, with her daughter, and her grandson.

"Did her daughter look familiar to you?" he asked.

"I don't really remember…it was so long ago. I just barely saw them for a few minutes then I was out the door."

"Well…the daughter you met is my daughter, and that was my grandson with her," he finished.

"What…I don't even know what to say regarding that!" I struggled. For the first time in a very long time, I was almost speechless. "How long have you known this?" I asked.

"Not very long," he answered.

"Does the daughter know?"

"No, she just thinks I'm just an old friend of her Mom's."

"Good grief, Jimmy! She is older than Jim...but Phyllis is older than her!" I struggled with the logistics as I tried to figure out where this other daughter fit into Jimmy's history.

"I know," was all he could offer.

"How and why did this happen, and why did she keep this a secret?"

"I can only guess the answer to that." He said. "All she told me was she got pregnant before Toni and I got married, and by the time she figured out that she was pregnant, I was already married to Toni. She was afraid if she told me, I would insist that she have an abortion, and she was never going to do that."

"So how did she keep this a secret all these years?" I dared to ask.

"She married some guy right away and passed the child off as his. This guy was no dummy and he quickly figured out that she was not his daughter, so he divorced her and did nothing to help with the support of the little girl," he went on.

"Why didn't she let you know then? It's tough trying to support a child by yourself. At least you could have contributed financially."

"She decided that it would be best if she just kept quiet and raised her child alone with only the help of her family," he continued.

"What would you have done if she had come to you and said that she was pregnant? Would you have insisted that she have an abortion?" I quietly asked.

"At that time I probably would have insisted that she have an abortion, but I would like to think that I would do differently now," he said.

I just continued to sit there quietly and let him unburden himself.

"Once I held my own children, my grandchildren… your children and grandchildren…it really made me regret all those abortions," he continued. He went on to say that he had never thought of those abortions as 'little people' with talents, and futures, and gifts that could be shared with the world.

It was difficult to hear all of that knowing how much my children, grandchildren, nieces and nephews have always meant to me. I could not imagine my life without any one of them, and I secretly wondered about the ones I would never know. I could not help but think of all the babies worldwide that had been aborted and what wonderful gifts they might have contributed to our world. At one time, I considered myself a 'pro-choice' person. I believed that a woman had the right to decide if she wanted to bring a child into the world or not. After all, it was her body, right? I don't believe that anymore. I now understand that God knows every one of those little souls before they ever enter their mother's wombs, and He has a purpose and a plan for each one of them.

"Maybe that's why I have worked so hard for the Shriner's Children's Hospital over the past years. I'm trying to make up for all the damage I've done in some small way," he sighed.

I knew the answer before I ever asked, "Did Mom have any knowledge of any of those abortions?"

"No way! You know how she felt about abortion!"

I could just tell by the sad look on his face and the tone of his voice that this was a regret that he would carry to his grave.

He and I discussed his daughter's existence again in depth when he was preparing his final draft for his will. He did not include her in anything…not that she needed anything from him, but I could just tell that he felt uneasy about the whole situation. To make matters worse, Marie died a few months after he revealed all this to me and as far as I know she never said anything to her daughter about who her real father was.

Sometimes in my grief, I felt like I was carrying the weight of the world on my shoulders. Usually, I tend to over analyze simple everyday issues, but these things were not simple. These issues were more than life or death issues. These were 'eternal' issues that I was burdened with and I was struggling daily with them.

Chapter Sixteen

Wolves Howling at the Door

As I continued on my journey back to God, my life continued to move forward. Sometimes, I just wanted to stop it all and just crawl into a dark hole and never come out, or lock myself away so that I didn't have to communicate or interact with anyone. Oh, I don't mean to imply that I wanted to commit suicide or anything like that. I just wanted to be left alone to contemplate all that my heart and my head was trying to reconcile. I just knew that eventually I would be able to sort through all of this and force it to make sense if only I could be left alone and not distracted by daily life.

In the meantime, Mike was working very long hours then spending over two hours every day commuting to and from work. Unfortunately, his income did not justify the aggravation he was enduring. The wolf was not just howling at the door now. He was gaining entrance! By the late summer of 2009, we were financially devastated.

Mike had continued to send out resumes and he networked all over the country, but up until this point nothing had helped in his quest for a better job. Nonetheless, we had continued to pray that "God would send us to exactly where he wanted us to be."

Suddenly, one day Mike received a call from someone he knew in Houston. He was looking for a General Manager for an RV dealership. Mike couldn't wait to get home and tell me about the call. He made arrangements to go out for the interview and check out the situation. Sometimes, these type of job opportunities can be a dead end opportunity, or worse yet a desperate attempt by an owner to bring in what they hope will be a 'miracle worker' to turn their business around and save it from dying. Mike had done exactly that a couple of times in his career, but he wasn't that young, driven man anymore. Besides, the current economy was probably the reason that this dealership wasn't doing well, not because of bad or inefficient management. Because Mike had been an automobile dealership owner at one time himself, he knew how to look beneath the surface to find the real problems lurking there.

Consequently, he went out to Houston, in good faith, to check out this situation and found that this was most likely someone that was looking for a 'miracle worker' or a 'magician', but we decided that maybe God wanted us back in Texas. Besides, this was more in line with his past career experiences even though it was a significant reduction from his previous executive salaries. At least it was a salary! Mike worked out the details with his new employer and made the decision to take the motorhome and leave immediately for Texas to start working. My job was to stay there in Florida, tie up all the loose ends, and join him within the next month or so. For some reason, we have always had one foot in Texas and the other in Florida, so our families were not the least bit surprised when we told them we were going back to Texas.

Mike started his new job with the motorhome parked right there on the premises of the business. He didn't seem to mind because he was practically working 24/7 anyway. It was nice to have a regular income again and see the hemorrhaging of money slow down a bit. He didn't complain, but I could tell that he was working himself to death every evening when we spoke. He needed me there with him.

A month later, I wrapped up all the loose ends in Florida, said my good byes to the family, packed my car, and got my cats ready to travel. Florida seemed like a huge 'ghost town' to me anymore. Everywhere I drove, I saw empty businesses that had thrived for decades, empty commercial properties boarded up, homes abandoned, and nice cars sitting in parking lots with 'for sale' signs on them. This was not the Florida that we knew. Thank God He was leading us along another path.

My children and my mother-in-law were concerned about me making that sixteen hour drive alone, so every couple of hours my phone rang with one of them questioning my progress. Other than the occasional interruption to talk to them, or the gas and bathroom break, I think I prayed and talked to God the entire way there. I reminded Him that Mike and I had nothing left...we were broke...our credit was ruined...we were not young anymore...starting over again at 63 was not as easy as it once was.

Mike and I had achieved considerable success and wealth three different times in our lives, but somehow we just could not seem to hold on to it. On that trip back to Texas, God made me understand that the reason we could not enjoy lasting success and peace was because we never gave Him the proper praise and Glory for all the blessings He had showered down on us. We thought we were responsible for it. Wrong!

I began to understand that we came into this world with nothing and we were going to leave that same way. God, in His generosity, had allowed us to be stewards of His blessings, but they never truly belonged to us or accumulated because of us. We are expected to accept those blessings and use them to bless the lives of others. Mike and I had failed miserably in that respect! When I fully understood that simple truth, I felt so ashamed and unworthy of God's forgiveness and grace.

I wish I could end my story here with something as blissful as, 'they lived happily ever after,' but that's not how real life works. The job that Mike accepted did not turn out to be what he was promised. We had many more financial difficulties, and Mike was not getting any younger, so job possibilities were not that plentiful. Even through all of that, we thanked God every day for bringing us to this wonderful area of Texas. I believe He did answer my prayer, and He led us to 'exactly where He wanted us to be.'

We made the decision that we would start going to church and try to learn more about God and His plan for our lives. We found a neighborhood church that we started attending which led to volunteering and getting involved in all sorts of activities and groups sponsored by our church. We met many new friends who shared similar experiences on their way back to God, and we met many that had lived truly God filled lives and were visibly blessed because they had. We quickly learned that life is a journey. In the past, we had chosen to make that journey without God, but now we were choosing to walk with Him every step of the way. One of my favorite scriptures became, *"For I know the plans I have for you, plans to prosper you and not harm you, plans to give you hope and a future" (Jeremiah 29:11).* I believed God's promise with all my heart.

Chapter Seventeen

God's Purpose Fulfilled

By the second anniversary of Jimmy's death, November 8, 2010, I was no closer to understanding how he had managed to return to bring me a message than I was the night that it happened. I'm ashamed to admit it, but I fully expected him to return that night and give me some kind of assurance that he had completed the work that God said he needed to do. Sadly, that did not happen. In the days and weeks that passed, I continued to hope that he would return or at least I would receive some kind of 'spiritual' sign that he was all right now.

It took me a while to understand that God's purpose had been fulfilled by Jimmy's visit. God owed me no explanation of what goes on in His Kingdom or anything else for that matter. Obviously, Jimmy's visit had caused me to humble myself before God asking for His forgiveness and accepting His Grace and Mercy. I will never understand why God went to such great lengths to save my soul, but over time I became aware that His message was not just for me. That little voice inside that nagged at me from the very beginning was becoming louder and louder. Somehow, I knew that I had to share my story with others.

Very tentatively, I started talking to people close to me about Jimmy's visit. To my great surprise, no one thought that I was mentally ill or delusional. About the worst remark I heard was, "Jayne, you were just dreaming! No one comes back from the dead." I just smiled at that remark knowing in my heart that I most certainly had not been dreaming and Jesus Himself came back from the dead!

Most people live their entire life without witnessing a miracle. Truthfully, most of us would not recognize a miracle if it happened right before our eyes! Until this happened to me, I was certainly in that category. Consequently, it took me a while to actually grasp the magnitude of this event. Even after I fully understood the significance of this experience, the analytical side of me still needed to break this all down into something that I could explain or rationalize in some way.

Right or wrong, I sat about trying to analyze and understand Jimmy's visit and everything that he said to me that night. The first thing that I needed to come to terms with was the very fact that my deceased brother had somehow been able to stand in front of me and deliver a message that he said was from God. Everyone, including the most spiritually separated person, knows that Jesus, the Son of God, rose from the dead. *"The Son of Man must be delivered into the hands of sinful men, be crucified and on the third day be raised again."* (Luke 24:7) *"This is what is written: The Christ will suffer and rise from the dead on the third day,"* (Luke 24:46)

To my amazement, I found other instances in the Bible where people came back from the dead. One such story is that of the widow's son found in (*Luke 7: 11-16*) *"Soon afterward, Jesus went to a town called Nain, and his disciples and a large crowd went along with him. As he approached the town gate, a dead person was being carried out-the only son of his mother, and she was a widow. And a large crowd from the town was with her. When the Lord saw her, his heart went out to her and he said, 'Don't cry' Then he went up and touched the coffin, and those carrying it stood still. He said,*

'Young man, I say to you, get up!' The dead man sat up and began to talk, and Jesus gave him back to his mother. They were all filled with awe and praised God. 'A great prophet has appeared among us,' they said. 'God has come to help his people.'"

Another such story is that of Jairus's daughter found in *(Luke 8:51-56).* " *When he arrived at the house, of Jairus, he did not let anyone go in with him except Peter, John and James, and the child's father and mother. Meanwhile, all the people were wailing* and mourning for her. 'Stop wailing,' Jesus said. 'She is not dead but asleep.' They laughed at him knowing that she was dead. But he took her by the hand and said, 'My child, get up!' Her spirit returned, and at once she stood up. Then Jesus told them to give her something to eat. Her parents were astonished, but he ordered them not to tell anyone what had happened."

The story of Lazarus, a more widely recognized story from the Bible, is further proof that people have returned from death. *(John 11: 39-44)* "Take away the stone," he said.

"But, Lord," said Martha, the sister of the dead man, "by this time there is a bad odor, for he has been there four days."

Then Jesus said, "Did I not tell you that if you believed, you would see the glory of God?"

So they took away the stone. Then Jesus looked up and said, "Father, I thank you that you have heard me. I knew that you always hear me, but I said this for the benefit of the people standing here, that they may believe that you sent me."

When he had said this, Jesus called in a loud voice, "Lazarus, come out!" The dead man came out, his hands and feet wrapped with strips of linen, and a cloth around his face.

Jesus said to them, "Take off the grave clothes and let him go."

To my well-meaning friend that suggested I had merely been dreaming the night that my brother visited me, I would like to remind her that the Bible shows us that God's power has no limit! I know that my brother actually returned that night, if only for an hour, to glorify God's name.

The next issue I decided to tackle was the two beings that assisted my brother as he entered and exited my bedroom. The Hebrew name for angel is "mal'ach" which means messenger. Perhaps they were angels that had been assigned the task of assisting my brother in delivering his message to me.

Angels are mentioned approximately 117 times in the Old Testament and approximately 182 times in the New Testament. We do not know exactly when God created Angels, but scholars theorize that they were created after the creation of the heavens, and before the creation of the earth because the '*angels shouted with joy*' upon its creation. *(Job 38:1-7)* "*Are not all angels ministering spirits sent to serve those who will inherit salvation?*" *(Hebrews 1:14)* In *(Luke 24:37-39)* Jesus said that spirits do not have *flesh and bones* as He had when He was resurrected.

Angels almost always appear as males with one possible exception found in (*Zechariah 5:9*) "*Then I looked up—and there before me were two women, with the wind in their wings! They had wings like those of a stork, and they lifted up the basket between heaven and earth.*" They are usually described as handsome males clothed in white robes. Most often though, there is no description given at all for the angel being referenced in a particular scripture.

In my search for an explanation for these spirits, I found several references to these dark 'shadow' figures in more modern times. The most interesting one came from one of our founding fathers himself. George Washington wrote in his 'prayer journal' a detailed report of a vision he had while at Valley Forge. The entire entry is extensive, so the following is just a small excerpt from that document. He wrote, "I beheld standing opposite to me a singularly beautiful being." This beautiful being was accompanied by an angel that Washington went on to add, "At that moment I beheld a dark shadowy being, like an angel, standing, or rather floating in mid-air, between Europe and America. Dipping water out of the ocean in the hollow of his hand, he sprinkled some upon America with his right hand, while with his left he cast some over Europe. Immediately, a cloud arose from these countries and joined in the middle of the ocean. For a while it remained stationary, and then it moved slowly westward, until it enveloped America in its murky folds. Sharp flashed of lightening gleamed through at intervals, and I heard the smothered groans and cries of the American People." The article referenced that 'dark shadowy' angel several more times in Washington's account of the vision.

    This account was given to Wesley Bradshaw, a writer, in 1859 by an old soldier who had been present with Washington in Valley Forge when this vision occurred. Bradshaw published it in the U.S. war veterans paper *"The National Tribune"* in December 1880. That paper later became known as the *"The Stars and Stripes"* which reprinted the article again sometime later.

All of my research confirmed to me that the beings that accompanied my brother were some type of angels that had been assigned the task of assisting him in delivering God's message to me. In the weeks and months that followed, I continued to analyze the entire experience, hoping that I would find some measure of peace that could tell me that my brother was now in a good place. In other words, that he had found eternal peace with God.

Chapter Eighteen

My Mother's Bible

In the meantime, Mike and I became very involved with our church and our new community. We were so blessed to find a church that offered anything that a person could possibly need on their journey back to God. Not only does our church have a lead pastor, but we are blessed to have several others as well. They offer something we call 'Life University' which is a roster of Bible study classes that are quite in-depth and detailed lasting an entire semester. The class discusses and analyzes scripture with almost the same microscopic intensity that a college level theology class would. This, too, was part of God's plan for us. He knew that I needed answers, and He knew that I would be able to find those answers and so much more right where He led us.

We also started volunteering with an organization started by our church before we arrived there which includes 32 other churches in our community that get together and do various services for the needy and underprivileged in our community. We have repaired roofs, cleaned yards and lawns, painted, scrubbed, collected food donations and just about anything else that one can imagine and loved every minute of it. I hardly recognized us anymore!

Then one day, I was going through boxes and found something that had belonged to my Mother that I had completely forgotten about. It was her Bible with the homemade covering that she had made for it decades ago. Tucked inside of her Bible was several old church bulletins, some scripture notes, and a poem that apparently held significant meaning to her. It was *'Footprints'* by Mary Stevenson: *One night I had a dream—I dreamed I was walking along the beach with the Lord and across the sky flashed scenes from my life. For each scene I noticed two sets of footprints, one belonged to me and the other to the Lord. When the last scene of my life flashed before me, I noticed that many times along the path of my life, there was only one set of footprints. I also noticed that it happened at the very lowest and saddest times of my life. This really bothered me and I asked the Lord about it. "Lord, You said that once I decided to follow You, You would walk with me all the way, but I have noticed that during the most troublesome times in my life there is only one set of footprints. I don't understand why in times when I needed you most, You should leave me."*

The Lord replied, "My precious, precious child, I love you and I would never, never leave you during your times of trial and suffering. When you saw only one set of footprints, it was then that I carried you."

I sat there sobbing as I read and reread this beautiful poem, and I knew in my heart that God meant for me to find this at this very point in my journey. I thought about all the 'trials and suffering' my Mother had endured in her life. Her father had died when she was only two years old and as a result of her Mother's poor decision, she had been denied the education and daily comforts that were her birthright. Her Father had been a teacher who had just been accepted into the seminary when he was stricken with the flu that eventually took his life at a very early age. Although she was only two years old when her father died, she never saw her grandparents or aunts and uncles again.

Then at the very young age of seventeen she met and married my father, who had more than his fair share of scars from his own childhood. She lovingly brought seven children into this world counting each one as a new and unique blessing from God. My mother's faith always led her to take each child as he or she was born and christen them in a ceremony at the church. With all her heart, she dedicated each one to God trusting that He had a plan for each one of us and that by doing this simple ceremony she was confirming to God that she trusted Him and whatever His plan might be for each child. Not once did my father join her in those ceremonies, but she never failed to do it.

She endured the total destruction of her home by fire, the diagnosis and death of her oldest daughter due to epilepsy, the stroke that partially paralyzed my father rendering him unable to provide for his family ever again, and so much more. Through it all, my Mother held on to her faith and her love of God knowing that she would spend eternity with Him.

I began to see the scenes from my own life and see where God had been there at those times when I was either too young or too ignorant to know that He was there in complete control and carrying me through.

One of my earliest childhood memories was my aunt rescuing me from our burning home. One night while my father was passed out drunk, and my Mother, the twins, Miss Jewel, and I were all asleep in our beds our house caught fire and burned to the ground. Unfortunately, we lived so far out in the country that even if a fire truck could have gotten to us, there wouldn't have been a water source for the truck to use to extinguish the fire. My Father, Mother, Miss Jewel, and the twins all got out of the house as neighbors gathered outside to survey the scene of yet another tragedy in our lives.

My Aunt, my Father's only sibling, looked around, saw the twins, and asked, "Did Jayne and John spend the night at Faye's house?"

"Oh my God, Noooo!" My Mother screamed. "John is with Faye, but Jayne is still in there!"

My Aunt went racing into that raging fire and found her way to my bed. She scooped me up in her arms, and as we crossed through the doorway, I saw the ceiling cave in right on top of my bed engulfing it in a ball of fire. Yes, God was right there even then protecting me when I was completely helpless and vulnerable.

I remembered the times in my childhood when my Mother would collect us all and put us in the car in the middle of the night to escape a drunken rampage that my father was having. She would whisk us away somewhere in the middle of the night to protect us from our father, who was threatening to kill us all as he waved his loaded pistol around in the air! Yes, God was most certainly there and in control then.

I remembered the day when I overheard a conversation between Jimmy and my Father that had caused me to look at Jimmy in a whole different light from then on. As I hid behind the sofa, I heard Jimmy tell Dad that if he ever touched our Mother again or hurt any one of the four children left at home, he would have to answer to him. He even took the pistol away from him that he had so often used to terrorize us. Yes, God was there as well giving Jimmy the strength and conviction to stand up to a man that he also had feared his whole young life.

Then later as a young wife and soon-to-be mother, both I and my unborn child almost died as the result of a long and grueling labor that lasted almost twenty five hours. My son should have been taken by Caesarean, but for some unknown reason, the doctor chose not to do that. I fully expected to die at that time because I was almost the same age then that my sister, Faye, had been when she died. Somehow and for some reason, God saw both me and my son through that ordeal. Yes, God was there, and that son is now in medical school.

A little less than three years later, my second son was born without all the drama that the first child endured. He, however, came into the world with so many food allergies that he almost died several times before the age of two. It was at that time, his pediatrician was able to properly diagnose his food allergies which ended our unwittingly poisoning him with the foods we were feeding him. Again, God saw our family through that and our son is a healthy grown man now blessed with an incredibly beautiful musical talent.

I now fully understand that my daughter is a special gift from God. If God had not been there in control of my life, I probably wouldn't have this amazing young woman that I am so privileged and blessed to call my daughter.

For that matter, if God had not held me in the palm of His hand, I probably would never have met my wonderful husband of forty six years. We met purely as a result of divine providence and we both know that for a fact.

I could see God's intervention in the motor home trip to Long Island that could have ended both mine and Mike's lives instantly had we gone flying at 60 miles per hour under that low bridge in our motor home. For that matter, that night in the Arizona desert we could have been killed instantly by a semi-truck that failed to see us sitting along the highway broken down in the middle of the night. The melanoma event could have gone undetected for months because they were all on my back where I would have never noticed them until the virulent cancer had run rampant through my body. I became convinced at that point that there were probably countless times that God had wrapped me in His love and protected me when I failed to recognize or acknowledge Him. To say that I was humbled and ashamed would be a gross understatement.

I began to see with great clarity all the times in my life that God had been right there carrying me with 'one set of footprints in the sand.' I felt so humbled and so blessed that God had given me another chance. The lyrics of the old Kris Kristofferson song, *'Why Me Lord'* kept repeating in my head. *"Why me Lord, what have I ever done to deserve even one of the blessings I've known?"*

Chapter Nineteen

My Search For Answers

As my faith grew stronger day by day, I continued to search for answers in my analysis of Jimmy's visit. The next part that I tackled was the disturbing imagine of Jimmy morphing from his death bed image to the young handsome man he once was. My quest led me to *(I Corinthians 5:1-10) "Now we know that if the earthly tent we live in is destroyed, we have a building from God, an eternal house in heaven, not built by human hands. Meanwhile we groan, longing to be clothed with our heavenly dwelling, because when we are clothed, we will not be found naked. For while we are in this tent, we groan and are burdened, because we do not wish to be unclothed but to be clothed with our heavenly dwelling, so that what is mortal may be swallowed up by life. Now it is God who has made us for this very purpose and has given us the Spirit as a deposit, guaranteeing what is to come."*

Most Christians believe that between the time of our death and the time of resurrection we will spend that time in heaven in the presence of God in a spirit form, but I think that is just part of the story. Once Jesus has returned to earth and established His permanent Kingdom here, we will be given new bodies, even superior bodies to the ones that we had in our lifetime. We will be recognizable by God and to each other.

In *(I Corinthians 15:35-38) But someone may ask, "How are the dead raised? With what kind of body will they come?" "How foolish! What you sow does not come to life unless it dies. When you sow, you do not plant the body that will be, but just plant a seed, perhaps of wheat or of something else. But God gives it a body as he has determined, and to each kind of seed he gives its own body."* Our weak, sinful bodies that we inhabit here in this life are but mere seeds that will be used to resurrect our perfect, super bodies at our resurrection.

I am going out on a limb here and suggest that my brother was at an in-between place in his journey. Perhaps he was there because God used him to deliver the message that I needed to receive. The process was obviously not completed because I knew that I could not touch him. Jesus said to Mary when she returned to the tomb, *"Do not hold on to me, for I have not yet returned to the Father. Go instead to my brothers and tell them, 'I am returning to my father' and your father, to my God and your God.'" (John 20:17).* Remember, when Jesus was resurrected, he was touchable by the disciples. *"Look at my hands and feet. It is I myself! Touch me and see; a ghost does not have flesh and bones, as you see I have." (Luke 24:39)* He even spent days with his apostles doing all the things that all humans do like eating, drinking, walking, and sleeping. *"And while they still did not believe it because of joy and amazement, he asked them, do you have anything* here to eat? They gave him a piece of broiled fish, and he took it and ate it in their presence." (Luke 24:41-43)

In *(I Corinthians 15:42-44)* "*So will it be with the resurrection of the dead. The body that is sown is perishable, it is raised imperishable; it is sown in dishonor, it is raised in glory; it is sown in weakness, it is raised in power; it is sown a natural body, it is raised a spiritual body.*" When we are resurrected, God will turn our old, sickly, imperfect, sinful bodies into something that we cannot even imagine in this life. What a beautiful thought that must be for anyone that was born with a handicap or other deformity that they have endured all their life, or a debilitating illness that has robbed them of their happiness and joy.

The next thing on my list to analyze was the fact that Jimmy said 'he had a Message for me from God.' Before God destroyed the earth in a great flood, he spoke to Noah saying, "*...I am going to put an end to all people, for the earth is filled with violence because of them. I am surely going to destroy both them and the earth.*" (Genesis 6:13) From that scripture, we know that God has and does speak to us at various times. Sometimes, His voice is as small as that tiny little voice inside us that guides us to do things that otherwise we may never consider like that tiny little voice inside of me that has pushed me to share my story with others.

At other times God's voice, no doubt, can be loud and frightful as it was in *(Exodus 20:1-17)*. God called Moses to Mt. Sinai *and* spoke directly to him giving him the Ten Commandments. *"... When the people saw the thunder and lightning and heard the trumpet and saw the mountain in smoke, they trembled with fear. They stayed at a distance and said to Moses, Speak to us yourself and we will listen. But do not have God speak to us or we will die." (Exodus 20:18, 19)*.

Most notably, God sent His son, Jesus Christ, in the flesh to speak His message directly to us. *"Oh Jerusalem, Jerusalem, you who kill the prophets and stone those sent to you, how often I have longed to gather your children together, as a hen gathers her chicks under her wings, but you were not willing." (Matthew 23:37)*

The story of Jacob is another example of how God can deliver His message to us. Joseph was the son of Rachel and Jacob's favorite son. Therefore, his brothers were jealous of him. Jacob sent Joseph to check on his brothers who were in Shechem tending their flocks. When Joseph arrived, his brothers were not there, but he met a man in the field that asked him, *"What are you looking for?" (Genesis 37:15)* Joseph answered that he was looking for his brothers. The man informed him, *"They are no longer here. I heard your brothers say they were going to Dothan" (Genesis 37:17)* Joseph eventually found his brothers who in a jealous rage sold him to a passing caravan as a slave. Things didn't work out quite as they had planned because Joseph was taken to Egypt where he became Pharaoh's chief minister helping Egypt survive a horrible famine. When Joseph's brothers arrived in Egypt looking for food, they found the brother they had sold as a slave! No doubt, that one man had delivered a message from God when He sent Joseph to Dothan looking for his brothers. That one act set off a chain of events that led Joseph to helping see Egypt through the famine, to Jacob's family arriving in Egypt in search of food, the Israelites becoming enslaved, the birth of Moses, the exodus out of Egypt, and God delivering His Ten Commandments through Moses. God's messages may appear small and insignificant at the time like the man in the field merely asking Joseph *"What are you looking for,"* but that's only because we can't possibly see and know all that He has planned.

God has even chosen to speak to us through those that have died. *"God accepted Abel's offering to show that he was a righteous man. And although Abel is long dead, he still speaks to us because of his faith" (Hebrews 11:4).* The Bible has given us countless examples of God's desire to speak to us both directly and indirectly. His power of communication is not limited to some preconceived notion that we may have of His abilities. He is the Most High God, Creator of heaven and earth. Therefore, He can communicate whatever He wants to us in any way that He chooses. He chose to communicate His message to me through my 'big brother' perhaps knowing that would be the most effective way to reach me because all other attempts had obviously failed.

I don't know what made me ask Jimmy, "Have you seen God?" At that time in my life I was so separated from God that I was in total denial of His existence. Jimmy's answer to me was an agonizing, "Yes...and it was very trying." This is not surprising to anyone that has read *(Exodus 33:20)* which states *"...you cannot see my face, for no one may see me and live."*

My exhaustive research for a Biblical description of God that matched Jimmy's report was somewhat disappointing. Jimmy said that He was "beautiful, blinding, no words could describe Him." I did find a passage that described Him as *'dwelling in unapproachable light.' (I Timothy 6:16)* Perhaps that is what led Jimmy to describe Him as 'blinding.' The most endearing and simplest description of Him is *"God is love." (I John 4:16)* Jesus was the personification of that love. *"God is spirit, and his worshipers must worship in spirit and in truth." (John 4:24)* Perhaps the best description of God is a close look at His Son, Jesus Christ. *"Anyone who has seen me has seen the Father." (John 14:9)* Several times throughout the book of *John*, Jesus describes Himself as the *"I am."* He also told us that He is *"the light of the world" (John* 8:12). The Bible states that when we are resurrected and God has established His Kingdom, we will see His face, but until then, *"Now we see but a poor reflection as in a mirror; then we shall see face to face. Now I know in part; then I shall know fully, even as I am fully known" (1 Corinthians 13:12).*

My brother was never considered a man of eloquent speech. As a matter of fact, he always struggled to put into words anything that was emotional or sentimental. I can only imagine how most of us would struggle to put into words the beauty and majesty of the creator of all the breath taking beauty in our universe. I can't even find the proper words to describe one beautiful sunset sufficiently! No doubt, Jimmy realized that he did not have enough time to try to describe God to me so he simply conceded and said, *"No words can describe Him."*

His message told me that I had to stop denying God's existence. He said, "You have got to go back to the things we learned as kids...she was right. God is real and we do have to pay for our sins...You've got to ask for forgiveness for your sins and ask Jesus to come into your heart and save you if you want to spend eternity in heaven... He's the only way." In *(Revelation 1:8) "I am the Alpha and the Omega," says the Lord God. "who is, and who was, and who is to come, the Almighty."* Yes, God is real. He existed before anything else and He will be here in the end. *"...Before me no god was formed, nor will there by one after me...and apart from me there is no Savior." (Isaiah 43:10-11)* God sent His Son into the world to save anyone that would believe. *"For my Father's will is that everyone who looks to the Son and believes in him shall have eternal life, and I will raise him up at the last day." (John 6:40)* Jesus reminded us that, *"I am the way and the truth and the life. No one comes to the Father except through me." (John 14:6-7)*

"Where you are now is temporary...it's just a dream," was another comment that Jimmy made to me that night that almost went without analysis until I started really trying to figure out what his message truly meant. We all know that that our lives have a beginning and an end as evidenced by our birth certificates and eventually our death certificates. Our life experiences and the individuals we invite into our lives layer by layer become the sum total of our history here on earth. It was no great surprise to hear him say that our time here is temporary. *"...for we were born only yesterday and know nothing, and our days on earth are but a shadow."* (Job 8:9)

Before I received this message from God, I don't think I really quite made the connection how temporary and fleeting this life on earth truly is. From the home that burned to the ground when I was a child to some of the spacious and comfortable homes that I owned as an adult including the beautiful waterfront condo that we lost in the end, it took this message to make me understand fully that *"This is my Temporary Home."* That is the name of a song by Carrie Underwood that certainly resonates with me now. *"This is my temporary home; it's not where I belong.*

Windows and rooms I'm passing through; this was just a stop on the way to where I'm going; I'm not afraid because I know this was my temporary home."

I now understand that I am a child of God...a citizen of heaven. Nothing here on this earth is permanent or lasting. *"But our citizenship is in heaven. And we eagerly await a Savior from there, the Lord Jesus Christ, who, by the power that enables him to bring everything under his control, will transform our lowly bodies so that they will be like his glorious body."* (Philippians 3:20-21)

Chapter Twenty

My Journey Back to God

By this time on my journey back to God, I clearly understand that sin of any kind comes with a big price not just in the hereafter, but even in our daily lives. One sinful transgression can torment one for the rest of their life, but that isn't even the worst of it. Unforgiven sin can cause the sinner an eternity of torment! *"For the wages of sin is death, but the gift of God is eternal life in Christ Jesus our Lord" (Romans 6:23).* All a sinner has to do is confess his sins before God and ask for His forgiveness and he is forgiven. *"If we confess our sins, he is faithful and just and will forgive us our sins and purify us from all unrighteousness" (1 John 1:9).*

Jimmy said that I needed to ask Jesus to 'come into my heart' which basically means to ask Jesus to come into my life. *Jesus replied, "If anyone loves me, he will obey my teaching. My Father will love him, and we will come to him and make our home with him. He who does not love me will not obey my teaching. These words you hear are not my own; they belong to the Father who sent me." (John 14:23-24)* Jesus went on to say that The Holy Spirit sent by God would be with us to teach us and remind us of everything that Jesus taught while He was here on earth.

Basically, Jimmy warned me that I had to return to "all the things that our Mother made sure we learned as children." To hear him say those words really was a shock to me because he was the absolute last person that I would have ever expected to hear that from. When he was alive, he and I almost delighted in our ability to separate ourselves from the teachings we learned as children. We were heathens and proud of it! I see now how sad and pathetic that was.

Jimmy must have felt the need to warn me about Satan because he knew that I didn't believe in him either. As a matter of fact, the devil meant no more to me than the tooth fairy or the Easter Bunny! That sort of bogey-man concept had been left somewhere back in my young adulthood! To my Great surprise, I learned that Satan is as real as The Most High God. Jesus said, "*...the devil is like a roaring lion prowling the earth looking for unsuspecting, weak people to devour.*" *(1 Peter 5:8)* Jimmy, to my surprise, had almost quoted that verbatim. My disbelief in him certainly made it easy for him to attack and destroy me. Knowing all that I now know and understand, that one fact quite honestly scares me to death! *"Be self-controlled and alert. Your enemy the devil prowls around like a roaring lion looking for someone to devour. Resist him, standing firm in the faith, because you know that your brothers throughout the world are undergoing the same kind of sufferings. And the God of all grace, who called you to his eternal glory in Christ, after you have suffered a little while, will himself*

restore you and make you strong, firm and steadfast."
(I Peter 5:8-10)

Revelation 12 tells us of the war that was waged in heaven between the Archangel Michael and Satan. Satan had been one of God's most beautiful and loved angels, but he was jealous of God. He wanted to be God. (*Ezekiel 28:17*) *"Your heart became proud on account of your beauty, and you corrupted your wisdom because of your splendor. So I threw you to the earth; I made a spectacle of you before kings."* Satan, with the support of one third of the angels in heaven went to battle against Michael. Of course, Satan lost and was cast out of heaven along with the angels that sided with him. *(Revelation 12:7-9) "And there was war in heaven, Michael and his angels fought against the dragon, and the dragon and his angels fought back. But he was not strong enough, and they lost their place in heaven. The great dragon was hurled down—that ancient serpent called the devil, or Satan, who leads the whole world astray. He was hurled to the earth, and his angels with him."* Unfortunately for us, Satan and his demons fell to earth where he has had full reign ever since. *(Revelation 12:12)* *"...He is filled with fury, because he knows that his time is short."*

No doubt Jimmy himself had been a victim of Satan. He knew first-hand the damage that Satan could cause an 'unsuspecting, weak person.' Satan tormented Jimmy throughout his life causing him a lot of misery and pain. Satan presided over the destruction of his marriage and family, and watched with glee as the most important relationships in his life dissipated and crumbled. I now understand that we must respect Satan and never underestimate his ability to wreak havoc in our lives. *(John 8:44) ...for he is a liar and the father of lies."* We must be able to recognize him. *"And no wonder, for Satan himself masquerades as an angel of light"* *(1Corinthians 11:14)*

Most importantly, we must resist Satan. I now understand that Satan had been lying to me my whole life. He had me convinced that God didn't care about me or my family. He had me convinced that I knew better than God. He even had me convinced that my plan for my life was much better than the plan God had for me. Therefore, the only way to effectively resist

Satan is by putting on the 'full armor of God.' *"Submit yourselves, then, to God, Resist the devil, and he will flee from you." (James 4:7)*

That night when Jimmy visited me he said "there are things that you cannot possibly understand now." For a period of time, I took that statement to mean that I could not understand so many things because I had not yet died, or not yet stood in front of God to be judged, but as I studied my Bible and researched more, I began to understand that Jimmy was also referring to my lack of knowledge of God's word and even my separation from God. *"I have much more to say to you, more than you can now bear." (John 16:12).* When Jesus died on the cross for our sins, a personal relationship with God was made available to each of us. By confessing our sins and asking Him to be our Lord and Savior, we enter into that personal relationship with Him. Jesus said *"But when he, the Spirit of truth, comes, he will guide you into all truth. He will not speak on his own; he will speak only what he hears, and he will tell you what is yet to come. He will bring glory to me by taking from what is mine and making it known to you. All that belongs to the Father is mine. That is why I said the Spirit will take from what is mine and make it known to you."* (John 16:13-15) Even though we are given full access to Him, we still have so much to learn. There is still an infinite amount of knowledge that we can never fully understand while we are here in this life. *"For my thoughts are not your thoughts, neither are your ways my ways."* (Isaiah 55:8)

When Nicodemus, a Pharisee, came to Jesus for answers, Jesus answered this way, *"I tell you the truth, no one can enter the kingdom of God unless he is born of water and the Spirit. Flesh gives birth to flesh, but the Spirit gives birth to Spirit. You should not be surprised at my saying, 'You must be born again.'* (John 3:5-7) I now understand that I have just scratched the surface of things that I need to understand about God and His plan for my life, and I feel certain that there are things that none of us will ever completely understand while we are still in these earthly bodies. *"Brothers, I could not address you as spiritual but as worldly—mere infants in Christ. I gave you milk, not* solid food, for you were not yet ready for it. Indeed, you are still not ready. You are still worldly." (1 Corinthians 3:1-3)

The most controversial, intriguing, and perplexing statement that Jimmy made to me that night was, *'He said I have a lot of work to do.'* As I stated before, nowhere in my Protestant upbringing could I ever remember anything suggesting that we get a second chance for salvation after death. Needless to say, this was a difficult concept for me to grasp until I started researching it. Let me begin by saying that I am in no way suggesting that I am some sort of scholar, biblical or otherwise, but I do have an inquisitive mind, and I was consumed with a burning desire to figure out what this meant and how I could reconcile it with what I had learned in my youth. After offering my disclaimer, I would like to share my findings on this topic. I only researched the four main religions found in our Western culture, Judaism, Catholicism, Protestantism, and Mormonism.

To begin with, both the Jewish religion and the Catholic religion have some sort of process for the cleansing of the soul after death. Both religions base their beliefs on writings found in the Apocrypha (which is a Greek word meaning 'hidden'). These writings were found in Bibles after the Fifth Century in a separate section between the Old and New Testaments and sometimes as an appendix after the New Testament. While some scholars believe they have great historical value, they occurred after the fulfillment of the prophecy, so neither Christ nor His Apostles ever referred to them.

The religious custom of praying for the dead is based on *(2 Maccabees 12:39-45; Revised Standard Version w/Apocrypha) "On the next day, as by that time it had become necessary, Judas and his men went to take up the bodies of the fallen and to bring them back to lie with their kinsmen in the sepulchers of their fathers. Then under the tunic of every one of the dead they found sacred tokens of the idols of Jamnia, which the law forbids the Jews to wear. And it became clear to all that this was why these men had fallen. So they all blessed the ways of the Lord, the righteous Judge, who reveals the things that are hidden; and they turned to prayer, beseeching that the sin which had been committed might be wholly blotted out. And the noble Judas exhorted the people to keep themselves free from sin, for they had seen with their own eyes what had happened because of the sin of those who had fallen. He also took up a collection, man by man, to the amount of two thousand drachmas of silver, and sent it to Jerusalem to provide for a sin offering. In doing this he acted very well and honorably, taking account of the resurrection. For if he were not expecting that those who had fallen would rise again, it would have been superfluous and foolish to pray for the dead. But if he was looking to the splendid reward that is laid up for those who fall asleep in godliness, it was a holy and pious thought. Therefore he made atonement for the dead, that they might be delivered from their sin."*

For the Jews, praying for the dead has been a custom since before the birth of Christ. They believe in a purification that takes place after death through a process called the Qaddish (which is derived from a Hebrew word meaning 'holy'). The following is an English Translation of the 'Mourner's Qaddish' which can only be recited with a quorum of ten Jewish men for the first eleven months after the death of a loved one and on each anniversary of the death (the 'Yahrtzeit').

"Glorified and sanctified by God's great name throughout the world which He has created according to His will. May He establish His kingdom in your lifetime and during your days, and within the life of the entire House of Israel, speedily and soon; and say, Amen. May His great name by blessed forever and to all eternity. Blessed and praised, glorified and exalted, extolled and honored, adored and lauded by the name of the Holy one, blessed be He, beyond all the blessings and hymns, praises and consolations that are ever spoken in the world; and say, Amen.
May there be abundant peace from heaven, and life, for us and for all Israel; and say, Amen. He who creates peace in His celestial heights, may He create peace for us and for all Israel; and say, Amen."

Oddly, in the Qaddish, there is never any mention of death or the deceased. Furthermore, reciting it for more than eleven months would be an insult to the deceased suggesting that their sins were so great that more time is needed for the purification of their soul.

The Catholic Church believes that purgatory "a place or condition of temporal punishment for those who, departing this life in God's grace, are not entirely free from venial faults, or have not fully paid the satisfaction due to their transgressions" (Catholic Encyclopedia) provides one last chance to pay for their sins. This concept is, like the Jewish Qaddish, based on *2 Macabees 12:39-45* which is not part of the Protestant Bible. The Apocrypha, which contains these hidden verses, was accepted at the Council of Trent in 1546 and became known as the deuterocanonical books and are a part of the Catholic Bible.

Catholics believe that purgatory is implicitly proven by the Biblical 'principle' that there is no sin in glory, therefore, between death and glorification there must be a purification point or purgatory. Explicitly they refer to *2 Macabees 12* mentioned previously *and "For no one can lay any foundation other than the one already laid, which is Jesus Christ. If any man builds on this foundation using gold, silver, costly stones, wood, hay or straw, his work will be shown for what it is, because the Day will bring it to light. It will be revealed with fire, and the fire will test the quality of each man's work. If what he has built survives, he will receive his reward. If it is burned up, he will suffer loss; he himself will be saved, but only as one escaping through the flames." (1 Corinthians 3:11-15)*

  The Catholic Church teaches that there is purification after death, and the purification process involves some sort of pain or discomfort, but God will assist those in the process in direct response to the prayers of the living.

  The Mormon religion on the other hand takes a little different view of the afterlife. They believe when a person dies his spirit is returned to God where he is reunited with loved ones that have also passed on. There in the spirit world they continue waiting for the resurrection, which is where their spirit and body are united never to be separated again. *"But Christ has indeed been raised from the dead, the first fruits of those who have fallen asleep. For since death came through a man, the resurrection of the dead comes also through a man. For as in Adam all die, so in Christ all will be made alive. But each in his own turn: Christ, the first fruits; then, when he comes, those who belong to him."* (1 Corinthians 15: 20-22) While in the spirit world they continue to work and learn about God and His plan for salvation. The conditions they find in the spirit world are directly related to how they lived their lives here on earth. If in this life they had not yet received Christ and His teachings, they will have an opportunity to do so in the spirit world. The Mormon Church does believe in heaven and hell, but hell is not a fiery hell filled with demons and unimaginable pain, but a separation from God and all of our loved ones for eternity.

Protestants believe that a person goes directly to heaven or hell when they die. *"Just as man is destined to die once, and after that to face judgment" (Hebrews 9:27).* *"Therefore we are always confident and know that as long as we are at home in the body we are away from the Lord." (2 Corinthians 5:6)* Protestants believe that Jesus Christ died on the cross to wash away our sins and by doing so all we have to do is repent and ask forgiveness for our sins accepting Jesus as our Savior ensuring that our souls go directly to heaven upon our death. Protestants see no need to downplay the sacrifice that Jesus made on the cross by suggesting that it was not sufficient to purify or pay for our sins. Jesus proclaimed, *"It is finished."(John 19:30).* By His sacrifice on the cross, we were given the gift of salvation. Even though none of the Protestant religions teach the concept of purgatory or a purification process after death, many well-known Protestants have openly embraced it. Every believer must look into their own heart and decide for themselves where they stand on this issue.

Chapter Twenty-one

Lessons Learned

It has been four years since the death of my brother and the anniversary of his visit with me. I guess I have matured enough in my understanding of God's word to realize that I will never see him again here in this life, but I still think of him almost daily and I still feel the void in my heart left by his passing. I don't think the sadness will ever go away, but at least now, I seem to smile more instead of crying when I remember him or something he said or did. Secretly, I admit that I still pray for him. What could it hurt, right? Somewhere along the way I decided that a dying persons last moments are very private before they take their last breath and pass from this world, so even though they may not be able to communicate on a conscious level, God is still able to communicate with them. One thing I know for an absolute fact, God is capable of anything that He chooses to do!

It has taken almost four years to write this story that I believe God wants me to share. While it has been painful reliving the loss, it has also been cathartic, but most importantly, it has been humbling to see how merciful God truly is. I've discovered that this isn't just a story about my brother returning after his death to deliver a message to me from God, but a story of my journey back to God which probably would have never happened had God not chosen to perform this incredible miracle in my life. The message that my brother brought was right in front of me the whole time. God didn't have to go to such extremes for me to get 'the message,' but, then again, maybe He did, and I will be eternally grateful that He finally got my attention and pulled me back from the edge of the abyss.

The Bible is full of God's words and messages to each one of us. All we have to do is *"...seek and you will find; knock and the door will be opened to you." (Luke 11:9)* In my studies and research, I have discovered that God loves us no matter what we have done or how long we have wandered in a 'spiritual desert.' He wants to forgive us our sins and welcome us home just as the prodigal son was welcomed home by his father. *"He is patient with you, not wanting anyone to perish, but everyone to come to repentance" (2 Peter 3:9).*

I have also learned that God does not always say "yes" to us. Sometimes, the things that we want the most, or the things that we think we need may not fit into the plan that God has for our life. He truly does know better than we because he can see into all of our tomorrows, and He knows if a particular situation fits with His plan for us.

The most important thing that I have learned on my journey is that God does have a plan for our lives. *"Before I formed you in the womb I knew you, before you were born, I set you apart"* (Jeremiah 1:5) All we have to do is trust Him enough to follow that plan.

Even in our darkest times, He is still there waiting to be the light that guides us through that difficulty. We need only to keep our eyes focused on Him and our hand firmly placed in His.

Mike and I are still right here in the wonderful little community in Texas that God led us to. We have learned and grown so much through all the situations and opportunities that God has placed in front of us. We have witnessed His miracles at work in our daily lives as He has guided us through so many financial difficulties, the loss of loved ones, and the challenge of various illnesses and injuries. Materially, we have less than we have ever had in our adult lives, but we are happier than we have ever been!

We are very active in our church and our community, and we have made so many wonderful, loving friends that have helped us on our journey back to God. We have reconnected with people from our past that meant so much to us, but for whatever reason (probably Satan) we chose to disconnect from them.

My biggest regret is that we waited so long to humble ourselves before God allowing His will to be done in our lives.

My personal vow has now become that I will never again let someone that I love and care about leave this earth without knowing that they have asked God for forgiveness of their sins and asked Him to be their personal Lord and Savior.

If I could have just one more minute with my 'big brother,' I would thank him for bringing me that 'personal message from God,' and waking me up to the perils that most certainly awaited me when I left this world. Who knows, maybe that was part of the work that God said he had to do.

Last, but not least, I thank God daily for all that He has done for me. He took this empty, broken shell, the most unworthy in His kingdom, and used me to glorify His great name. He has given me the incredible honor of sharing my story with anyone that will listen. I have no idea what God's plan is from here, but I do know that He is in complete control and I trust Him completely. Only God knows if I will see my 'big brother' in heaven, but just imagine the happiness and joy I will feel when I can run to him and throw my arms around him and hear him say, "See, I told you I would always be your big brother!"

About The Author

Jayne Schriver was born in a sleepy little cotton mill town on the Georgia-Alabama border in 1948. She was the fifth of seven children, raised in a blue collar family, but went on to achieve academic success at Florida State University where she graduated with honors.

In 1966, she married her husband, Mike Schriver, and started her life as a full time Mom of three, and eventually, grandmother of four. As of this date, she has been married to Mike for 46 years.

Although her first play was written at the age of 12, she never dreamed of publishing any of her work. Writing was something that she always aspired to do, but until now, never felt that she had a story compelling enough to share with others.

Jayne is currently very active in her church and community in Katy, TX where she and Mike both volunteer for countless projects and activities. She is a member of the Daughters of the American Revolution, an Eastern Star, a member of Phi Theta Kappa, and Beta Gamma Sigma.

www.ingramcontent.com/pod-product-compliance
Lightning Source LLC
LaVergne TN
LVHW011416080426
835512LV00005B/91